G000136796

——— ADVANCED ———
MOUNTAIN BIKING

ADVANCED
MOUNTAIN
BIKING

DEREK PURDY

SBL
Springfield Books Limited

© Derek Purdy 1994

This edition first published by
Springfield Books Limited, Norman Road, Denby Dale, Huddersfield HD8 8TH,
West Yorkshire, England

This book is copyright under the Berne Convention. All rights are reserved. Apart from any fair dealing
for the purposes of private study, research, criticism or review, as permitted under the Copyright,
Designs and Patents Act 1989, no part of this publication may be reproduced, stored in a retrieval system,
or transmitted in any form or by any means electronic, electrical, chemical, mechanical, optical,
photocopying, recording or otherwise, without the prior written permission of the copyright owner.
Enquiries should be addressed to the publishers.

First edition 1994

British Library Cataloguing in Publication Data
Purdy, Derek
Advanced Mountain Biking
I Title 796.6

ISBN 1 85688 040 0
ISBN 1 85688 046 X

The author and publishers would like to thank the following for the use of copyright material: Map
symbols from Landranger, Pathfinder, Outdoor Leisure maps by the kind permission of Ordnance Survey
© Crown Copyright; The British Mountaineering Council for the first aid information in Chapter 12;
Mountain Biking UK for the use of the navigation illustrations on pages 82-87 and 91-94

Photo Credits
The author and Publishers would like to thank the following photographers:
Steve Behr for the photos on the frontis and pages 42 (left), 44,71 (lower), 72, 73, 107, 108, 126, 143 and 144.
Adrian Gidney for the photos on page 30, 31, 97, and 105 (upper).
Paul Watts for the photo on page 117. All other photography is by Derek Purdy

Design: Design/Section
Illustrations: Paul Tudor
Printed and bound in Hong Kong by Colorcraft

Dedication
This book is dedicated to all lovers of mountains and bicycles

Contents

Introduction

There is a lot more to mountain biking than riding. Bike skills are very important, and you couldn't get out there without them, but having achieved a high level of competence in the handling department the door opens to greater things. In fact there is virtually no limit.

Advanced mountain biking encompasses the full spectrum of conduct and survival in the hills, respect for the environment, confidence to navigate through new country, and above all, enjoyment. The thrill of just being there, watching an old heron gliding through the setting sun, the croak of the raven accompanying you on a tough plod to gain a high col, or simply marvelling at a morning cloud inversion as you enjoy the first brew of the day. It is all there for the taking.

We'll see you on the hill.

DP

Foreword

I was standing in a muddy field in the North of England at a mountain bike race. I was supposed to be commentating, but since the organiser was Derek Purdy I didn't actually have a lot to do. Rather than set up a race on the normal format of a few laps of a bunch of pine trees Derek had arranged a huge 18 mile loop that everyone, no matter what the racing category, was to ride just once. In mountain bike racing this was an iconoclastic, almost heretical move, but the racers came back grinning from ear to ear and the only complaints were from the really fit lads and lasses who had wanted to be out on the Northumberland moors for longer, and from a commentator who had

felt a bit foolish sitting in front of a mike for almost two hours with no riders visible to commentate on...

To Derek mountain biking has always meant more than just racing and short rides in the woods, so with hindsight a maverick race format was no real surprise from him. He's been galumphing up and down mountains, on feet and ropes and in rally cars, for longer than this whippersnapper has been on the planet. Over the years he's shared his hard-won knowledge and experience of the mountains with Mountain Biking UK readers, and I'm delighted to see his mountain experience distilled into a book.

Most of us who come to mountain biking from the road or

the sofa have little in the way of the techniques needed to read maps properly, navigate safely in the mountains and 'read' the terrain we're riding across. There are lots of books that cover these techniques but they tend to cater for the pedestrian needs of fell walkers and mountaineers.

Mountain bikers are different; we travel more quickly (well, most of the time) and we have more fun doing it. If you want to extend your enjoyment beyond your local trails and into the real mountains, this book is a must.

John Stevenson
Deputy Editor of Mountain Biking U.K.

Chapter 1
Getting Started

Bike choice

Virtually anything can be ridden over the hills, but it's a great help if you've got the right kit. Charles Freeston published his *Cycling in the Alps, A Practical Guide* in 1900, and while these early touring cyclists followed the roads of the day they were no more than mule tracks in most places. Their bicycles had elevated footrests, so it seems fair to assume that they were riding fixed wheel and these additions were a means of resting their legs up out of the way of the flailing pedals. We have come a long way since then.

My personal introduction took place in 1958. I was loitering in Seatoller, in the middle of the English Lake District, not really fancying the eastern side of the Honister Pass, when a much older unacquainted cyclist invited me to accompany him across Styhead. My protestation that there was no road fell on deaf ears, and we set off. I was told this was 'pass storming', the old diehards had been doing it for years, some even with tandems, but in all fairness I either walked or carried my FC Parke's lightweight 98% of the way. It was enough, I was hooked, and I've been doing it ever since. Needless to say I've done a lot more of it since the invention of the mountain bike, and unlike some of the elders of the rough stuff fraternity in the British Isles I embraced the mountain bike and am eternally grateful to Messrs Fisher and Richey for their invention.

Intended use

If you are about to upgrade your steed, or even launch into mountain biking for the first time, consider what you intend to do with the bike, and where you intend to go. If you intend to go farther, higher, and probably carry extra load in the shape of camping equipment, your bike will get some serious hammer, and a model from the cheapest end of the market will not survive.

Unless you buy an end of season bargain, you are unlikely to get a suitable bike for less than £400 (or 500 dollars) at 1994 prices.

Unseen factors like the quality of steel used in the frame and axles are important. Under load you'll find the back axles bend regularly unless they are good quality. Brazed on bosses for pannier racks and mudguards make fitting so much easier.

Of course you may need to upgrade your existing bike, but make a detailed list of what you need, then price all the items carefully.

On most occasions you'll probably find it makes more sense to buy a new one!

Go to a dealer who has a good selection of bikes in your price bracket and asks questions like Where are you going to ride? What will it be used for? and How much can you afford? The 'Just have a look around' brigade are unlikely to be as well informed, and if you expect them to make time to talk to you, which they should, don't go on a Saturday morning when the place is jumping, go mid morning mid week.

Size

The right way to size a mountain bike is to stand over it with your feet on the floor. It is right for you if you have three or four inches clearance between the top tube and your crotch. My road bike has a 23-inch frame, my mountain bikes are 18.5, need I say more? There are so many times when you come to a stop on very rough terrain when you need to put your foot down and there's nothing there, when it happens you'll bless your smaller frame.

Younger riders are especially prone to the 'grow into it' attitude. Please don't do it. I know regular replacement is an expensive exercise as children grow, but it is absolutely necessary if you want to be grandparents. There is a thriving secondhand market in mountain bikes, so it is probably not as bad as you think.

Another aspect of sizing is reach; it's often neglected. Correct reach is difficult to judge. Too long a reach, usually due to too long a bike is usually obvious, but too short a reach can be awkward and restrict your breathing. You need the right length so that you can use all of your upper body strength effectively – especially on the uphills. The only true test is to actually ride the bike.

Many dealers will let you test ride

the bikes, more should; ideally there'll be an off-road test area nearby, and you will need to leave a substantial security like cash, driving licence, cheque cards, or even a hostage, but it could be a good way of getting rid of the wife! If you go when it is really quiet one of the staff may well come out with you to make sure you don't abscond and may even give you advice.

Hiring

One of the best ways to test ride a bike is to hire it. Good hire centres in mountain districts usually have a fleet of off-road bikes that have got to be good to stand up to the treatment they get. Couple this to a sales outlet with a good aftersales service and you have an excellent arrangement. Hiring is also an excellent introduction for you or a friend you want to entice into the sport, but don't go over the top.

Don't try to climb Everest on your first time out. Choose something like a forest trail, or an old road or well-used track where you'll spend 90% of the time actually riding. The tougher challenges come later.

Bike preparation

Riding higher usually means remoter too, fewer people, fewer chances of assistance with

breakdowns, farther to wheel or carry should anything break. Bike bits do get broken: caught on a rock, entangled in heather, jammed by a stick, or they simply wear out or suffer metal fatigue. You can minimise these risks with first-class maintenance and preparation. Don't try to make things last one more trip, if it needs replacing do it now. We've all tried to stretch the life of bits and paid for it with a walk back, don't do it.

Any maintenance is time well spent, cleaning, oiling, greasing are all worthwhile. Apart from anything else they familiarise you with every aspect of your bike, and you should spot any ailing accessories before they let you down in some remote place. Work your way through the *Checklist* regularly – at least once a month.

Setting it up

Saddle adjustment

Probably the most obvious single factor in matching you to your bike and certainly one of the most important parts that should be set up correctly is the saddle. There are three elements to it, height, fore and aft adjustment, and tilt.

Good saddle adjustment is paramount, it is critical to proper pedalling and efficient use of your

Checklist

Part	What to look for
Tyres	Pressure, cuts and abrasions, cords fraying, brake block contact, wear, thorns and flints
Wheels	Running true, spokes loose, bent or broken
	Bearings, cones, adjustment and lubrication
	Quick release skewers, lubrication
	Rims, dents and wear. They do eventually wear out, especially in winter
Brakes	Adjustment, cantilever bolts Check cables are lubricated, not frayed (replace even if only one strand is broken), tight in clamps particularly on new bikes after a couple of months use, free in straddles free in outer sheaths. Grease guides where bare cables enter, check bottom bracket guides have not been crushed.
	Check blocks are clean, correctly aligned (slight toe-in) have plenty of wear remaining
Bottom bracket	Lubrication, adjustment, lockring tight
Crankset	Crank bolts or nuts tight, nuts being especially prone to working loose, chainring bolts tight, damaged teeth (straighten then file off burrs), excessive wear or hooking and running true
Pedals	Lubrication, adjustment, damage, cage bolts tight, toeclips and straps OK
Chain	Cleanliness, lubrication, wear
Rear changer	Adjustment, cleanliness, jockey wheel wear, cable fraying, lubrication
Front changer	As rear changer plus clampbolt tight
Freewheel	Clean, lubricated tight
Thumbshifters	Lubrication, damage
Brake levers	Clamp bolts, lubrication, cables
Headset	Adjustment, lubrication
Handlebars	Clamp bolt, stem bolt, bar end bolts tight. Grips in good order
Saddle	Bolt, seat clamp, tears
Water bottle	Boss bolts. Cage distortion or cracks

energy. Admittedly there are people who use the most bizarre saddle positions and seem to do very well, but are they an odd shape, or would they do even better if we could convince them to analyse their position? For the rest of us time spent setting up your seat can prevent a sore bum, and other injuries too, as well as making you a more efficient rider.

Height: basically it is the same as any bike, when you sit on the saddle and engage the pedals your knee should still be slightly bent at the bottom of the stroke, not locked out, The sort of angle your legs would adopt if left

Saddle positions — right and wrong. Left: (a) Too high at the front, Centre: (b) Too low at the front, Right: (c) Correct. You may prefer it very slightly raised at the front, but not as much as at (a)

to hang loose. Likewise at the top of the stroke your thigh should never quite reach the horizontal position, if it does then your saddle needs raising.

Once you find your ideal height, mark the seatpost by scratching a line or making a single spot with a centre punch so that you can find the position easily in future. It is not unknown for a seatpost to wiggle its way down during a particularly long and bumpy descent, especially if the bike is new. This will also give you instant relocation after cleaning and greasing which is a worthwhile exercise if you do a lot of winter or wet riding.

Many seatposts have a limit line near the bottom, never raise the post above this line: it keeps a safe amount of post in the seat tube to support your weight. If you need to exceed this you need either a longer seatpost or a bigger frame.

Fore and aft adjustment: the technical school of thought decree that correct positioning should be arrived at by sitting with your feet on the pedals, the pedals level, then adjusting the position until the line down from your knee to the pedal axle is vertical. Alas I can never remember whether it is the front of the knee or the middle, and resort to the comfort system.

Comfort is what you should aim for, not only in saddle positioning but in any aspect of mountain biking. You are going to take a pounding by going farther and higher so anything you can do to make it more comfortable is always worthwhile. Start off with your saddle positioned mid-way on the saddle rails, the two bars underneath the saddle which run through the seatpost clamp, and see how it feels for pedalling and reaching the handlebars. This adjustment is a personal thing related to your preferred riding position, if you like to be stretched out no doubt you will move it back which effectively lengthens the top tube of your bike, on the other hand if you like to be on top of things you may well move it forward, but mid-way is a good starting point for virtually every shape of saddle.

Tilt: nearly everyone who rides seriously has their saddle level, or tilted back very slightly, that is with the nose of the saddle slightly higher. Good quality seatposts always have micro-adjustable clamps to help you achieve your ideal position, and once set tight it should never move. If it does, take a very close look at your seatpost, it may be bending!

Stem height and reach
Obviously the position of your saddle both in fore and aft adjustment and in tilt can affect your stem adjustments. A forward tilting saddle will throw your weight forward with resulting numbness in your fingers and genitals and excessively aching wrists, so do all these adjustments together, and then be prepared to refine the settings

after a ride or two.

The handlebars should generally be a couple of inches lower than a horizontal line from your saddle. This should see your back at an angle of about 45 degrees.

Stem height is easy to adjust. Simply loosen the Allen key quill bolt and slide the stem up or down in the steerer tube. Again there is usually a limit line on the stem, don't exceed it, and be prepared to adjust your brake cables. By raising the stem you might still be able to apply the brakes, but lowering the stem will leave so much slack they might not work at all. Check before riding.

Most mountain bikes come with stems which have a reach of about 130mm, which are much better than earlier models which were about 100mm, although ladies bikes still seem to come with short extensions for some reason. Riders have gone from sitting bolt upright to leaning further forward which gives much more control, particularly at speed, and many manufacturers have responded by lengthening the top tubes.

For those who like a line to start from there is the nose setting. Imagine a vertical line from the tip of your nose, or even tape a plumb line on your snout, when sitting in your normal riding position with both hands on the handlebars. Sporting, or dare we say it aggressive riders, will like a line directly down

to the quill bolt. More novice or laid-back riders will prefer a line a couple of inches behind the quill. If the line falls in front of the quill you are on a bike that is too small for you, if you are more than a couple of inches farther back you are sitting too upright and will have trouble on uneven ground, the front of the bike will bounce around.

Bar ends are a great way of giving you more choice in positioning and greater leverage. There are dozens of different shapes from dead straight to whole auxiliary handlebars, and all have their devotees, but all provide alternative positions for the hands and less chance of fatigue and numbness as a result. Once tried they are seldom deserted. One disadvantage is that they stick out at the front so they tend to catch on branches in confined situations. The effects of this can be minimised by using an inwardly curving design which not only virtually eliminates the problem but affords a degree of protection for the hands.

Setting the controls

This is fine tuning, but it's just as important for longer and more arduous trips. Integral systems such as Shimano's Rapidfire give you no choice because the shifters and brake levers are interconnected, but work very well indeed. Separate thumbshifters and brake levers can be positioned where you want them.

Brake Levers: hold your hands out in front of you as if you were holding the handlebars. Look at the angle of your fingers, they'll be slightly downwards. Set your brake levers to suit. There will be occasions when you need maximum leverage on your brakes because it is wet and muddy, or even icy, and the angle becomes more exaggerated downover when you stand up – and you **will** be braking standing up – so set the levers at about 45 degrees and fine tune them from there.

Thumbshifters: take a lead from the integral systems, see how close coupled they are. You need to be able to change gear without moving your hands away from the grips and to be able to push away through all the gears with your thumb and then return with your forefingers. If you run out of thumb on the last couple of gears they are too far away. Start with the tops horizontal and tune them from there.

Special considerations

Longer days in, and out of, the saddle demand some special considerations and little deficiencies that can easily be tolerated for a couple of hours become major problems on long days and extended tours.

The following suggestions are borne of experience, some of it quite bitter!

Saddles with a sealed surface are a must. Whilst it's accepted that even with mudguards the saddle is going to get wet, at least with a sealed surface the moisture will run off, and when conditions become drier such a saddle might even help to dry saturated shorts by squeezing the moisture out as you ride. By contrast fabric coated saddles tend to hold moisture with uncomfortable results. A good gel saddle is a sound

Fabric coated saddles tend to hold moisture with uncomfortable results. On the morning of the fifth wet day of a 250 mile route, Glenn Wilks takes desperate measures in an effort to start the day with a modicum of comfort!

investment for prolonged off-road journeys. Tropical travellers often advocate leather saddles because they breathe better, a major factor when you're dripping sweat day after day.

Grips should be of rubber or firm sealed cell foam to repel water and not deform too much on long

descents. This was brought home to me in no uncertain terms in the Val di Fossa, Northern Italy, on the descent from the Eisjochl or Passo Gelato, 2895m. The two-hour downhill deformed the grips to the point where they would have come off the handlebars if bar ends hadn't been fitted.

Trackmitts are a necessity as they offer more padding and more shock absorption. Leather and foam are best, some of the gel types lose their effectiveness after a while when the gel shifts to one end of the palm pad.

Suspension units will add weight to your bike, but there is no doubt that any form of suspension will limit fatigue. There is a terrific range of suspension forks available: the Girvin Flexstem is quite effective for a limited weight gain, my personal preference are the PACE RC-35 or the Shocktechs because of their light weight and reliability of their elastomer spring/damping medium. Although the best recommendation for front suspension came from Jane Simpson, prior to the Great Australian Bike

Race. Dawes supplied her and husband Bob with a Double Edge tandem fitted with Rockshox which they first used on the 1992 Welsh Polaris Challenge. Jane told me the bike was more comfortable and stable than anything else they had ever ridden, and she was only half as frightened on the big loose descents as she normally is!

Toeclips are another essential item. If you don't use them now get a pair and get used to them. Don't do them up tight initially, in fact they work very well with a setting whereby you can slide your feet in and out at will, and you'll fly away from the bike with ease should you crash. Detaching is easy, just pull up and back together and your foot will come out. Once you get used to clips you might like to try the more advanced Shimano SPD system, which is really impressive as far as foot location is concerned. It can be a bit exciting if you need to walk over wet rock as the cleat area gives you little or no grip, and in very cold conditions the shoes are useless when wet, your feet freeze. A demon tweak for the toeclips is to fit buttons or pulls to your straps, they help you to tighten your clips which is what they are designed for, but more importantly they act as a stop and prevent the strap being pulled right through the buckle by heather when negotiating very wild terrain.

Lights on mountain bikes aren't as daft as they sound. Long days in the saddle, particularly in winter, can often lead to you coming off the hill in the dark, not the best idea in the world but we've all done it! Many mountain passes in the Alps, or even the ordinary roads in Norway or the Faeroe Islands, have lengthy tunnels so it is as well to be prepared.

For night time off-road riding and winter training a good rechargeable set-up, although initially expensive, is a sound investment. Twin headlights are a must to give a good spread of light and angled so one will give distant illumination in case fallen trees are encountered (more bitter experience!), and even a third light pointing down not very far ahead of the front wheel is a useful fill-in when you get into the adventurous stuff. Obviously the larger capacity batteries will be physically bigger too, but my Peppiette System uses a 20 Ampere Hour battery which fits into a cannibalised water bottle, which in turn fits into a bottle cage, and gives about four hours riding using twin headlights with 2.4 watt bulbs. This is more than adequate. The battery takes about 12 hours to recharge fully.

Top of the list in the weight/ effectiveness/universal uses category is the Petzl headtorch. Whilst not strictly legal in the British Isles, and no doubt in many other countries, for road use because your front light should be attached to your bike, it is

Twin headlight setup. The battery is contained in a cannibalised water bottle and gives about four hours light with two 2.4 watt bulbs. The advantage of a twin headlight system is that one beam can be set slightly higher than the other to give either a more concentrated light just in front of the bike, or cast a longer beam to give earlier warning of distant hazards

perfectly adequate for riding on-road, it follows your eyes whenever you turn your head off-road, and is truly excellent around camp. Wonderlight also make a similar kit but I still prefer my Petzl Zoom, I've never had to test it, but I feel that it would perform better when signalling for help with alternative pencil and wide angle beam sequences.

The lightest/most effective rear light currently available is the Vistalite which uses light emitting diodes (LEDs) instead of bulbs and two small high power 1.5v batteries which give well over a hundred hours of light. Again despite their practicality they are technically illegal because they flash, but they are very effective. Most models

come with a belt clip so your bike is not encumbered with protruding brackets when the light is not in use.

Mudguards are necessary for winter riding, in fact some riders seem to measure the quality of a route or a day out by how dirty they become. Tracks don't dry out so well in winter due to the lower sun, shorter days and cooler temperatures, then when the snow melts they still run with water. I usually fit my mudguards in October and keep them on until April. They really do help on two-day tours. Lightness freaks will no doubt only use front protection, probably in the shape of a Crud Catcher, which at 66gms has got to be weight effective.

Bottom Brackets are best kept bathed in grease. Riding through a lot of water plays havoc with your bottom

Conventional mountain bike mudguards work very well in most conditions, but they do need clearing from time to time. The latest innovation from Pete Tomkins is the Crudguard. Rubber mounted, virtually indestructible, and highly effective

bracket bearings. By sealing all the frame tube holes at the bottom bracket assembly, and fitting a grease nipple and filling with grease, you can keep them practically waterproof. Water still gets in a little, but is expelled when you pump in the grease periodically via the nipple. The small amount of water that still gets into the tubes can be drained out by hanging the bike up at odd angles from time to time.

Weight is of paramount importance for longer and tougher days and tours. Whatever you fit and carry always think about how it changes the weight of your bike, it really does make a difference.

Extra equipment

For higher routes there are some additional items worth carrying:

A Whistle could save your life and weighs very little. It is also very useful for calling back the greyhounds who press on beyond shouting range, and want to take the wrong route when you have the map! For the recognised Mountain Rescue Signals see Chapter 12.

First aid kit is a good idea if there is a party of any size, but it may seem a bit over the top as a personal item. Boots Chemists do a tiny kit which

is quite good, including a couple of antiseptic wipes and a pair of scissors which get used for all sorts of jobs, but it doesn't contain all my prerequisites. However, the minimum you need is a small roll of sticking plaster that can also be used to repair bags, clothes, glasses, and a small tube of antiseptic cream – it's amazing what a dab of cream can fix.

Survival Blanket which should be aluminiumised on both sides, then it will keep body heat in and also reflect excessive sun just in case you need it in the Sahara. A friend of mine did and it worked.

Don't unfold it until you need it, they never go back as small again, they are a 'use once' item, but who's counting, in an emergency use it.

Spares your preparation should reflect your confidence. A spare inner tube should suffice, otherwise where do you stop? Anything may break at any time. I know someone who has carried a spare seat clamp bolt for five years because he had two break in quick succession, but I don't know anyone else who has ever broken one. Be reasonable. All my tools and spare tube (plus my Polaris shell jacket!) go into a small bag fastened under the saddle. Trek bags excel in this department, they come in a terrific range of shapes and sizes, and are all amply endowed with Velcro fastening.

Emergency rations such as PowerBars should be available and easy to get at in your luggage. If the seal is unbroken they will keep for at least a year. A sachet of your favourite electrolytic drink is also useful but you should be drinking this all the time anyway. The old standby is Kendal Mint Cake 'As supplied to numerous Everest expeditions'. You either love it or hate it. Like the incredible Bolland Brothers I love it, in fact we use it quite frequently as a measure of a route's difficulty. No route can officially be described as an 'epic' unless mint cake was eaten!

Tool kit

A mountain biker should be self sufficient in the hills for both themselves and their bike. Sharing the tool kit can ease the load but make sure **you've** got what **you** need, there is no point in blaming someone else when you're up there and find yourself without, you may need that tool. Your tool kit will reflect the level of your preparation.

I have mixed feelings about the compressed CO_2 cartridge and the humble pump. I always carry a pump because it will inflate an infinite number of tyres, but slower. The compressed gas cartridge inflates the tyre instantly but will only do one. The Superflate Speedpump allows controlled release of the gas, but you'll still probably use the whole canister for a flat. Another disadvantage reveals itself in cold, damp weather, substantial amounts of frost form on the cylinder as the gas is discharged and can freeze your fingers to the unit. You then look a right prat lying at the side of the track breathing heavily on the whole lot to release yourself. Their great advantage is speed. Most of the racing fraternity now use them, but also when you're out on the hill vital minutes saved when you're running before a storm or seeking help could make one well worth it.

Tool kit checklist
- Pump
- Small adjustable wrench
- Suitable selection of Allen keys
- One tyre lever – something else will double as the other one, the handle of the wrench for example
- Chain splitter – your chain might not break, but you may have to shorten it if you wreck a rear mechanism
- Puncture repair kit, in case you get two or more punctures, and if you're going to get one you'll get two
- Piece of soft wire – 1001 uses
- Spare toe strap – use it as an auxiliary tie for the under saddle toolbag
- Pair of mini pliers – they really help if your hands are frozen

Bumbags

Without doubt the best and most popular way of carrying the rest of your bits and pieces on a mountain bike is the bumbag. Unlike walkers who seem to have an ongoing competition to see who can carry the most, you should travel as light as possible, but certain items are essential.

Checklist
- Survival bag or blanket
- Mini first aid kit
- Coins for emergency phone call
- Emergency rations (see above)
- Food
- Whistle
- Map
- Compass
- Pen/pencil
- Pump, if it isn't strapped to your bike
- Camera

This lot should fit into any reasonably sized bumbag. My personal preference lies with the expanding type: they give that extra capacity to accommodate the extra layers of clothing you shed on hot days, or the little treasures you may collect along the way such as mushrooms, blackberries, apples, sheep skulls or antlers. Among the best are Forme 4 by Outbound, and the faithful Ellis Brigham expander. I have used the latter on a daily basis for the last two years and found it excellent.

Top: the Ellis Brigham expander bumbag has a good capacity, while allowing the garments on your back to breathe at their optimum efficiency.
Bottom: the Ellis Brigham fully expanded

Depending on where you live and ride, the terrain will vary enormously, even opposite sides of a hill or valley can consist of different soils, and opposite sides of a mountain although composed of exactly the same rock can present different problems due to the lie of the strata. A fine example of this is the extreme northern end of the Pennine Chain on the old coffin road that lies between Garrigill and Kirkland. The climb westwards from Garrigill is mainly gradual and slabby, but this changes as soon as you ride over the col. The western flank is much steeper and you are constantly dropping off the ends of the slabs, like steps, which is hard on

the wrists when descending, but virtually impossible to ride up. At least that's my excuse for getting off!

Some soils particularly at lower

Where running water combines with the erosion caused by agricultural vehicles, ruts can assume gigantic proportions, but this section of the Captain's Road, Selkirkshire, Scotland, still has a generous helping of frogspawn

levels, encourage a lot of growth with tree roots intruding into paths and tracks. Invariably they lie at an angle producing awkward little bumps when dry, and making lethal slides when wet. Fallen logs, very easy to see and tempting to negotiate either by leaping them or by hopping the front wheel over and driving the rear over with a mixture of rear wheel and chainwheel, are equally as lethal. Hit them straight on, regardless of the landing on the far side. I have painful recollections of a very greasy specimen lying straight across a track in Mabie Forest, Dumfriesshire. Approaching at a reasonable speed I

Occasionally roads that lie lower than the surrounding countryside degenerate into two ruts because the surface is often covered with water. This example, on Morleyhill Fell, Northumberland, is usually a pair of water filled troughs, supporting a fine selection of aquatic plants and a fantastic number of frogs at the appropriate time of year

saw a deep gulley, accentuated by the path, immediately beyond the log, I decided that the ground to the left of the hole was a better option and deviated from my straight approach. The result was the back wheel shot along the log instead of over it, and my right leg was up around my head somewhere before I crashed down half on the trunk half on the ground. The mark the tyre left on the barkless log was about two metres long, rubber, moss and dampness are obviously a very slippery combination.

Riders who have motorcycle trials or enduro experience take to mountain biking so easily, in fact many of them use it as part of their fitness programme. The reason they do so is because they read the road so well, the enduro boys have been doing it much faster, so the speed attained on a mountain bike is no problem. You will soon develop this skill if you constantly take notice of the state of the path and the type of terrain you are traversing. You can relate or link various factors to anticipate track-borne hazards. Here are a few examples:

- Laneside trees - roots, twigs, leaves on track
- Farmyard muck heaps - slippery droppings or slurry
- Harvesting - mud on road, tractors around the bend
- Hedge trimming - high puncture

possibility, especially if hawthorn
- Fallen leaves - lethal on stones, also hide holes
- Streams crossing tracks - soft sand, mud or detritus
- Regular water on stony tracks - moss or ice
- Blocked moorland drains - sphagnum stopper
- Sandy or peaty soils - deep gullies in soft ground
- Wooden bridges or duckboards - lethal when wet
- Stalkers tracks - four-wheel drive ruts, dips full of water
- Shaded areas in winter - surprise ice
- Old woodland - fallen trees at any time

Start by consciously linking terrain and hazards in an area you know well, and build from there. You've probably been doing it subconsciously since you started biking but by thinking about these factors you'll stand less chance of being caught out in strange territory. What you may think you may never be able to anticipate are the manmade hazards like the wooden drainage channels set into Highland stalkers tracks, but once you've seen one on an estate you'll know what to expect thereafter. In fact you'll be looking to see which method they employ, will it be the single plank system, the fabricated wooden channel set into the road, or the stone culvert

which is also a favourite in Lakeland, and can be a serious obstacle.

Your catalogue of potential hazards will become enormous, but so will your knowledge of the countryside and your appreciation of rural craftsmanship with the use of readily available materials.

Rough ground

What do you call rough ground? It is all relative, and depends upon what you are used to and accept as the norm. Even on one particular route there may be a rough section, or what you consider to be a rough section, which someone else may negotiate without giving it a second thought. The other side of the coin is the situation where you don't even notice a rough bit because it is well within your capability and skill range, but some other poor soul may be bewildered by the whole thing. Bear this in mind, particularly when taking novice riders out, what to you might be easy, to them could be their biggest challenge yet.

Where you live will colour your impression of rough ground too. Norfolk tracks are in the main sandy and smooth, whereas in Northumberland the peaty tracks are often punctuated by large stones, but visit the Isle of Skye and you'll find stones, boulders, slabs - the lot. Go farther afield to somewhere like the Annapurna Circuit in the Himalayas and you'll find most of the trails consist of rough flags; this is porters' and ponies' country where loose stones are easily disturbed by the hooves of yaks and ponies, rendering some stretches totally unridable. These trails take a heavy toll on porters' footwear, you see dead flip-flops and trainers everywhere, no wonder so many Sherpas travel barefoot.

Lesser trails the world over tend to harbour sharp stones due to the lesser amount of traffic, and some high altitude roads are subject to mud slides and catastrophic erosion. The hostile environment and the short period of the year that many mountain passes are open, means that paths are not surfaced. In wet conditions these can become rutted and very rough and even difficult to descend. Rough uphills can stop you, but, unless you are laden with expedition gear, they can be overcome. Occasions often arise when you need to heave your bike through rougher sections or even over large rocks. Obviously such situations require balance and strength, but it is amazing what you can ride through or over with practise and confidence.

While most off-road techniques demand gentle applications of strength and a lot of 'feel' for the terrain, these extreme sections demand extreme measures, a sort of instant on and off power response. You'll need to stand up to get the power you need, not bolt upright, a coiled spring stance, arms bent with a low back and room for powerful pedalling. Try to use a stop-start rocking motion, although you don't actually rock backwards, powering the bike over the bigger obstructions. Then, just when you are about to lose traction, plonk your bum on the seat for a split second to restore grip, then immediately hurl yourself forward and up again using all your upper body strength and both your legs, via the toeclips or shoeplates.

Elaine Hopley descending the Devil's Staircase towards Kinlochleven. Hard to imagine that this was the only road through to Fort William before the present route was driven down through Glen Coe to Coe village

Don't overdo the forward position otherwise you'll lose the grip you've just re-established, but with practise you should be able to synchronise your effort with your pedal stroke and possibly amaze yourself with the power you produce.

Wider tracks often degenerate into two ruts. Many are wide enough to pedal along with care, or to free-wheel, keeping the pedals as level as possible or favouring the highest side. Sometimes these stretches are prolonged and narrow. Half pedalling can help to maintain progress: as the name suggests you only turn the pedals half a revolution, or less in a deep rut. A high gear is essential; the quicker the recovery, or back-pedal phase the greater the chances of success.

Occasionally ruts become full of water, so on top of the width restriction there is deep water to negotiate. You can either walk around it or settle for becoming very wet!

Descending over rough ground is even more hazardous. You are invariably travelling faster, hit the hazard at speed, and have less time to choose a line. Paul Eynon, a follower of the 'faster the better' school of thought, is usually phenomenally successful, being the winner of the notorious Devil's Staircase Race, in Glen Coe, but I don't know anyone with a larger collection of bottomless shorts! Elaine Hopley, several times Scottish

Ladies Champion has a different philosophy, she flies down the good parts but slows right down and picks a delicate line through the boulders. She can even manage the metre-high rock step on the Kinlochleven side of the Devil's Staircase with her system, something which I have never achieved. It is not so much the step, as the boulder field beyond which is the danger, the consequences of a fall among the granite blocks would be horrendous.

In circumstances as extreme as this there is no disputing the value of suspension, as long as you don't go completely mad and finish by blowing the oilseals.

Tussocks

Tussocks are bunchy clumps of grass

found in the colder damper hills, or at lower levels as the latitude increases, or severely decreases. The Falkland Islands even have their own species *Poa Flabellata,* which grows several times larger than any found in Europe.

There are two types of tussock, soft hearted and hard hearted, they look identical and the only way to tell them apart is to ride into them. You'll only find them on lesser used ways but even the shepherd's quad tracks will avoid the worst.

The easiest way to negotiate them is to weave through, which is a messy business because they frequently stand, if not in water, in very wet mud or peat. Steer the front wheel between them, hope the rear wheel follows, but be prepared to stand up and let the rear end bob about behind you. If you are heavily laden you'll be forced to walk.

Tussocks invariably cover whole moors. Here Norman Canham, an enduro motorcycle rider of considerable experience, makes light work of threading a track together in the Cheviot Hills, Northumberland

Boggy ground

Bogs are called swamps in Equatorial latitudes, mires on Dartmoor, and every county in Ireland has its own extensive bog. East of Glen Coe, Scotland, lies the desolate moorland of Rannoch Moor, one of the most famous bogs in Britain. This glaciated area is a mixture of lochs and lochans, morainic and glaciated knolls, peat filled hollows and blanket mires. In many places the peat has eroded away to expose stumps of ancient Scots Pine, known often as bog oak, which have been preserved for several thousands of years. The Moor is crossed by a few tracks, it would be folly to attempt to cross it any other way. In fact there are many who would say it is folly to attempt to cross it at all!

Most of the bogs we encounter are relatively smaller but you will find them in any waterlogged area, and populated by plants which will tolerate permanently wet conditions. Predominant among these are the sphagnum mosses that will establish themselves quite substantially in a couple of years. They vary from bright green through yellow to straw coloured and brown, and some even turn red at certain times of year. Bright green is youngest and softest, brown is oldest and hardest. Sometimes when you are travelling through a boggy area you think the whole world is being taken over by this stinking morass, but sphagnum cannot tolerate industrial pollution and is virtually absent from the fringes of the larger connurbations.

Every county has its own type of bog, here Paul Eynon falls foul of a seemingly bottomless mire on the side of Loch Ericht, on the northern fringe of Perthshire, Scotland

Sphagnum moss is reputed to have medicinal qualities and was frequently used as a wound dressing during the Border Wars, but I can't help wondering if this was due to the fact that there was nothing else available, and am more likely to settle for something from the first aid kit.

Ditches and gullies that become blocked are ideal places for sphagnum growth, the moss grows level with the surrounding terrain, and before you know it you have a 'stopper'.

Soft enough to allow the front wheel to break through, but often dense enough for you to ride over or through without breaking open.

Unless the bog is new and only two or three inches in depth you will need a lot of speed or strength or both to make a successful crossing. If you take it gently you've got no chance at all, but the worst that will happen, **usually**, will be dirt up to your knees. I say usually, because I was involved in the rescue of a friend who broke through the crust of a sphagnum bog.

Three of us, including Steve Bell, were riding the ancient Broadway on Hexhamshire Common,

Sphagnum stopper Willyshaw Rigg, Northumberland. It wasn't posed, that's how the bike came to rest. If you start running as you come over the handlebars you can usually stay on your feet

Northumberland, in mid winter. There is an extensive bog beneath Hangman Hill, albeit under three to six inches of water. Steve was last man. Whether we had weakened the structure of the pad or whether he had taken a slightly different line I don't know, but when we reached the wettest and deepest part he broke through. We effected rescue, which seemed necessary at the time, by using his and my bikes for extra support, and learned a valuable lesson. If you are alone, ride around - no matter how far it is.

A large bog of these dimensions is unusual on the line of a right of way, the more frequent stoppers are only up to three or four metres width maximum, most a lot less. The most success is usually achieved by charging them hard keeping the front wheel as light as possible. There are two possible results: you get through, covered in bog, or, you fly over the handlebars as the front wheel digs in, but even then you may make the far side if you start running before you hit the sphagnum. The only problem is that you need to go back for the bike, which can sometimes take an awful lot of pulling out. Wet ground is soft ground and more susceptible to damage, although bogs seem to heal themselves immediately, especially over the winter period. Treat them with care.

Boulders

In terms of hardness, boulders lie at the opposite end of the scale to moss. In mountain biking terms anything bigger than a stone is a boulder, they are exceedingly difficult to negotiate and are a high risk damage factor. Glaciated areas worldwide are renowned for their boulders, rocks of various sizes that have been bowled along by the ice, rounded, and rendered virtually useless as building material; although there is an old track from Inverbain, Wester Ross, that linked Loch Shieldaig with Applecross that used boulders about half a metre diameter as the bed. Unfortunately the abundant rain has washed all the intermediate filling away over the years, and what remains is a track that is virtually unwalkable and impossible to ride. On many popular paths a combination of both natural and manmade erosion has left only the boulders. Rossett Gill, Cumbria, is an extreme example for which there is no easy solution.

Riding amongst boulders is a tiring process, there is a limit to how many boulders you can bunnyhop in a day, like none if you are heavily laden, and even weaving through them is risky. One rider squeezed neatly between two in Glen Sligachan, Isle of Skye, only to have the rear mechanism guard catch and break the end completely off the spindle causing a lengthy walk back.

Wheels can be twisted when trying to squirm through, so many folk advocate a head on approach riding up and over providing you don't damage the chainrings. If you regularly use trails where boulders abound protection to the chainring, such as an 'explosion bar' or Rockrings, may be a worthwhile investment.

Pedalling techniques will be

dictated by the size and frequency of the boulders. Level is a good starting point and allows you to get the power on as soon as you are clear, but you may have to rotate one crank as you pass one obstruction to clear another with the other pedal. Be prepared to make constant adjustment to avoid damage to your bike and yourself. Boulders present a substantial case for wearing boots as opposed to shoes.

Peat hags

A hagg, or hag, by definition is the rough overhanging edge of a peathole or stream bank, but can be extended to include any step of peat. In truth they can only successfully be ridden when either frozen solid or bone dry, anything in between presents difficulty. The degree of difficulty is directly proportional to the dampness. They are so soft that on many stretches of the Pennine Way boardwalks have been erected over the worst areas, which are great for mountain bikes if a bit lethal when wet. It is virtually impossible to ride up them but they can provide the ultimate practice ground for your drop-off technique. Dry conditions are best for obvious reasons, and the landings are soft apart from the heather twigs which seem to abound. Some hags are enormous, the bigger they are the

further back you need to be on the bike, over the back wheel with the seat in your stomach if necessary. Normally on drop-offs you must keep off the front brake altogether, but on peat you can risk a little retardation because the ground is so soft the front wheel will sink in sufficiently to give you steering until you virtually lock the wheel.

Mud

Mud is great. You can slip in it, slide in it, race in it, or even wear it as a trendy fashion accessory in certain quarters! On the other hand it can impede progress to the point where it is not funny. The worst conditions imaginable confronted well-travelled rider Simon Vickers on his crossing of Siberia. He learned the hard way that nothing moves in summer except by train in this part of Asia and spent three weeks pushing through filth and gloop on the remains of winter tracks which were submerged in water. Of course mud is not restricted to colder climes, Indonesia and Madagascar seem to get more than their share and Equatorial Africa abounds in the stuff.

There are so many colours and consistencies too. Variations from

good old fashioned mega-glutinous clay, which can set like concrete in summer or become puddled into a seemingly bottomless trough in wet weather, to the southern chalks which make you look as if you've had a really good day out, leaving you completely white, but the same stuff can come very close to ice when wet. Moorland mixes are usually black and peaty, less solid than their lowland counterparts but considerably more cunning.

A favourite ploy of the moorland mud magnet is to dress itself with a

Mud negotiation: watch the girls, they skip over the top, but when you hit a 20-metre stretch of the soft stuff, you need bit of bulk and a lot of power to force through

veneer of black peaty water, often barely covering the surface of the more solid matter and sometimes masquerading as a pool, but the main weapon is inconsistency. There may be three, four or even ten water covered splashes that you ride through with very little impediment, then bang! your front

The Crud Claw is an excellent little device which scrapes mud out from between the cogs. It only weighs 20g, but is worth its weight in gold when the going gets really sticky

wheel goes in up to the axle, doesn't even turn a full revolution and you are out the front door in a major way. There is no foolproof method of avoiding the occasional exit over the bars, despite every imaginable variation in speed, adjustments in attitude of the bike on approach and in transit, there is no guarantee of

success. Do what you think is best!

The major factors in negotiating mud are trailcraft, speed, rider weight, gear choice, tyre choice and technique and innovation.

Trailcraft

You will develop trailcraft through miles and miles of riding, but the following principles will help.

- Concentration is paramount. In slippery conditions watch what you are doing **all** the time, don't wander from the task for an instant, and if possible keep an eye on what is happening to others too.
- Observation follows naturally, look at the mud, look at the escape routes, look for alternatives, look for apparent changes in consistency the most obvious example being where a mud patch has dried at the edges but is still a pool of liquid in the middle.
- Anticipation: try to think how the bike will behave, and what will happen. You'll be surprised how often you are right.

Speed

Speed is very important. Mud of any sort impedes you, so the general rule must be that the faster you hit it the better chance you have of getting through. When you see mud coming up accelerate in the last 20 metres, attack it and drive through, **but**, and it's a big but, mud is

slippery and offers very little grip so changing line can be difficult. Sometimes the line is far from ideal, but success will be measured simply by whether you get through.

Rider weight

Rider weight affects technique, but has got to be a major factor depending on the consistency of the mud. It can work for or against you, so you are best off being average. In most muddy conditions the lighter you are the better, because you won't sink in so much. Watch the girls, they skip over the top, and also watch the sprogs, they hardly leave a mark, but also watch what happens when they hit a 20-metre stretch of the soft stuff. They haven't got the power to force through. So you need a bit of bulk and a lot of power.

The heavyweights needn't despair. In most cases you'll sink in so you'll need to choose a good line, probably near the edge, but you can use your weight to advantage. I once did a job for a magazine high on the Lakeland fells above Kentmere and came across a peaty stretch where the rushes had been flattened and recent rain water was running through. Obviously the fibrous nature of the rushes provided a lot of grip and prevented the bike sinking into the mud, but the water reduced their effectiveness. I felt that I needed that bit of extra grip and achieved it by bouncing as I executed the power stroke of the pedal.

The same thing worked 300 metres farther on at a stream crossing. The edges were eight to 10 centimetres deep with oozy black peaty mud, but the centre of the stream was stony and pebbly. Going in was OK but getting out was more difficult. It seemed reasonable to assume that there would be stones underneath the mud so I took my time, let the back tyre sink in a fair way, then applied the power in a controlled fashion while trying to keep the weight on the back wheel. Even sitting on the saddle I was able to bounce a bit and it worked, but my colleague, who is considerably lighter than me, got a wet foot . . . or was I just lucky?

Gear choice

When the going gets slippery ride as high a gear as possible. This is a principle that works with motorcycles and cars so why shouldn't it work with bikes. The theory is that in a high gear you produce less torque so are not as likely to spin the wheel, but this is one you will really need to work at. Only lots of experience will get you the right gear every time.

Tyre choice

The great debate. Basically the more open the tread the better the traction. Not only has there got to be enough bite there has to be ample room for the mud to escape or be thrown off. Ask 10 regular mud riders for their favourite tyre and you'll probably get eight different makes or models. Panaracer Smoke Lites are good, the Specialised Cannibal in either 2.2inch or 1.8inch works well, but the Highlanders seem to prefer the Specialised Storm Control which gives reasonable control in rocky terrain too.

To say the least, mud tyres can be interesting on tarmac, in fact when it is wet they can be lethal. Each has slightly different characteristics, you soon adjust, and all you have to do is slow down a little after all. Onza Porcupines grip very well in mud, so well in fact they wear out quite quickly, especially the white ones, and in common with all very open tread pattern tyres throw mud off as they clean themselves. Glasses help enormously in this department but so do mudguards or the even lighter Crud Catcher which is easier to fit.

Clearance between tyre and frame is important in glutinous conditions, particularly if you favour the widest tyres. Not only is mud deposited on the bridge behind the bottom bracket by the tread of the tyre, really sticky stuff often clings to the wall of the tyre not only adding to the build up but adding a lot of weight too.

It is worth stopping occasionally when conditions are this bad to scrape the walls of the tyres and clear the frame, and it helps to ride through any water you encounter to ease the situation.

If the situation becomes really dire, and you are forced to push for any distance, release the brakes, apart from making it easier it reduces the abrasion of the brake blocks and wheelrims.

Long before this, particularly in cold weather, mud is attracted to your chain and gear mechanism, often to such a degree that the rear block becomes choked and the chain begins to skip on the cogs. The plastic toothed Crud Claw is the answer to this problem. Invented by Pete Tomkins it's a simple but very effective device that mounts on the end of the back axle and simply combs the mud out from between the cogs as you ride.

Technique and innovation

Mud dictates modification of your normal riding techniques. On descents generally keep the wheels rolling, particularly the front, once you start to slide at speed all is lost. Keep your weight back a little so the front wheel is less likely to dig in, but not so far that you lose steerage. Keep moving, the quicker the better within reason. Brake early and gradually, you may need a couple of revolutions to clear the mud before you get any retardation at all. Locking up always causes a slide, mud can only accentuate it, but you can use the mud to your advantage by steering with your back wheel locked at the bottom of descents, and it is a means of negotiating hairpins, but don't overdo it. Climbing in mud demands all your weight over the back wheel. Just sitting in the saddle not standing up is pretty effective but a real thigh burner. Often it is only slightly slower to get off and push, sometimes even quicker, and always far less energetic.

Innovation often works. The Steve Bell system is to pull a wheelie at every puddle, it keeps his face clean but his back gets the lot. The Cooper-Parker approach is to try to leap the lot, frequently successful, but occasionally disastrous! Do what you think is best. Post-mud cleaning should be done as soon as possible after the ride before the mud sets, then re-lubricate thoroughly.

Sand

Sand isn't limited to the deserts, or the hot places. Without doubt they are the most spectacular in this sphere, but anyone who rides in a sandstone area will tell you of its abrasive qualities with regard to bearings, and its strength sapping

Often when a route lies through sand the soil has a clay content which binds the sand, or sufficient stones to make the route passable. It is still absolutely necessary however to stick to the track to limit erosion. Unclassified road at Iron Scars, Howick, Northumberland

element whenever you run into it. Usually whenever roads or tracks lie in sandy places the route follows an area which is not totally sand. Sometimes the ground has a clay content which binds the sand and makes it ridable, occasionally evaporation has left a good crust where it is possible to cycle or even drive on the top, and often there are sufficient stones to make the route passable.

Again your all-up weight will have a bearing on your progress because once you break through the crust there is no option but to stop, look for a firmer bit, and start again, gently. Sandstorms in desert regions, hot or cold, are desperate. The grains viciously attack every bit of exposed skin, so you must make provision because the bigger crossings may take you two weeks or more. Learn from the locals, don the Lawrence of Arabia gear. Even going to the toilet is horrendous. Sand can be ridden over, especially when it is frozen. In fact in such conditions it gives good grip, but that phenomenon is not often encountered, so make the most of it when you do.

Above: Moor Divock, Cumbria, Glenn Wilks forcing through wet overnight snow, not yet deep enough to cause problems greater than higher energy expenditure

Snow — well, actually it's not — in fact it's exceptional frost build up due to many consecutive nights of sub-zero temperatures. The going is very crunchy with excellent grip on Waskerley Way, County Durham

Snow and ice

It is possible to ride on snow and ice but only when it is compacted and frozen hard. Sheets of ice can be negotiated with great care but somehow it feels harder than concrete when you come off. Even the Alaskan Iditabike becomes the Iditapush for most of its 200 miles most years despite innovations like twin front wheels and studded tyres.

Siberian winters plunge to -40°C but well before then your brakes freeze up and you are forced to keep them full on to warm up the blocks and rims. As soon as you undertake any riding in snow or ice your brake block wear escalates, it must be the minute grit particles locked in the

Sheets of ice can be negotiated with great care and concentration, but in this instance at Hayeswater, Cumbria, things are approaching silly proportions. Windblown water, which can be seen flying off the top of the spillway, has frozen turning the ford and the surrounds into a skating rink

ice, and apart from the risk of stopping power the wheels become filthy making puncture repair a messy job. The wear rate can be such that a laden bike can consume a pair of blocks in 100 miles. Be prepared. From an amusement point of view glacier riding is difficult but possible with care. A suspension bike makes better progress on the ice, no doubt because it smoothes out the rider's

movements, but for serious crossings allow a walking timetable plus a bit for the awkward carries.

Due to brakes freezing up, as mentioned above, the most reliable retardation system when on the bike is literally sticking your foot out. Sitting on the crossbar will help in that direction, and you can swap legs to give your bum a chance!

Water

What sort of day is it? Would it be more sensible to avoid it? There are two definite approaches to water depending on the weather. No one minds a bit of water in the summer, it soon dries, but on cold winter or spring days it can add considerably to your discomfort, and is best avoided.

The golden rule is 'If you don't know it, don't blast it', in fact the super-sensible would say don't ever trust it. On one occasion, two of us were riding out towards Loch Ericht from Loch Rannoch on a reasonable forestry road punctuated by puddles one July day, the water being no problem at all, when my friend flew over the handlebars – a metre wide puddle had accepted half his front wheel. Quite unbelievable! No other pool had come up to rim height, and it was on an uphill too. You can never be sure.

Most of the water we ride through is puddles, water-filled ruts, or streams running across the track. Whatever it is hit it straight, you can slide on rocks or slabs which turn very mossy in summertime and they are the very best you can expect.

Stream or river bottoms are notoriously unpredictable because the water is constantly moving stones, rocks and waterlogged branches. Take care. Assessment is usually instant, on the run as you approach, but assess it nevertheless. Consider the following:
- if it is running, it is comparatively shallow
- if it is relatively smooth surfaced

Winter water can be deeper, will definitely be colder, so demands greater respect. This rider at Watendlath, Cumbria, has decided to remain seated to provide as much weight as possible for traction. The bridge was spurned because of very mossy rocks on the riverside path

Death or glory approach! Great fun if it is near the end of a ride and you don't mind getting wet, but even on a concreted ford there is always the possibility of hitting rocks or stones washed down onto the base by the current. Alex Spence charges the Wooler Water at Coldgate Mill, Northumberland

Death or glory approach II. A soft-bottomed, but familiar ford means a safe soaking and straight home now if it's a cold day at West Coldside, Northumberland

there aren't too many rocks
- rocks on the bottom always make the surface tumble or wave
- if there are tyre marks on both sides it is probably ridable
- if the surroundings are rocky, the bed of the stream will be rocky too
- if the track sees frequent use the moss will be rubbed off the stones in the bottom
- assess the exit, it could require a very low gear to get out.

Sill water runs deep. Sometimes very deep! In Alpine regions turbulent snow meltwater carries a lot of loose stones, bottoms are usually very loose. Assess the situation at major fords by riding along the banks if possible. (See also Chapter 11 River Crossings) Because of the uncertainty of any water and the splash factor, an out of the saddle stance is a good position to adopt, it gives a little extra height away from the water, an extra shock absorbing element, and instant power should you need it. Don't try to hammer out of water you will probably spin the wheels and end up as muddy as ever.

Chapter 3
Core Techniques

There are certain basic techniques essential to mountain biking that are similar to road cycling, one exception however is braking. On the road you mostly use the front brake; off-road, because of the looser surface you would mainly use the back brake. This chapter outlines the core techniques needed to deal with most circumstances, all you need to do is hone them to suit your style of riding. Don't be afraid to experiment or adapt any of them to combat the myriad different conditions you will encounter on the trail.

Downhilling

Racing downhillers now wear body armour: a good reliable helmet, long-fingered gloves, knee and elbow pads, leg and arm warmers and a one-piece upper-body motocross suit. While I am a great advocate of helmets, and always use elbow and knee protection in downhill races, somehow I can't see serious tourers going about the hills in all this kit, but the extra speed you generate on the dowhills certainly makes you think, and bear in mind the debris will be coming up at you faster so don't forget your eyewear. Extra weight in the shape of panniers and camping gear can increase your kinetic energy considerably with the proportionate increase in stopping distances. You'll not need any reminding of the potential after it has happened once, but the first time it occurs you'll think your brakes aren't working, when in fact they're probably on the point of bursting into flames. This is one of the main reasons for the appearance of disc brakes on MTB tandems.

The type of terrain dictates which of the different techniques you'll need to utilise, but the basics are as follows. Stay relaxed or even loose on the bike and let it do the hopping and leaping about under you, but not so loose that you could lose control if you hit an especially rough patch. Keep your body as upright as possible and manoeuvre the bike about underneath it. Watch the good trials riders, even the motorised men, some of their techniques seem exaggerated but it is usually the bike that's at the weirdest angle.

When cornering keep your weight on the outside pedal. This has two benefits. First your bodyweight will be more likely to be directly above the bike, and second the inside pedal will be further away from obstructions like rocks or the inside of a narrow track. Also be aware of the following:

- Avoid harsh use of the brakes. In technical sections try to keep off the front brake altogether. Brake before the corners; braking half-way around is a recipe for disaster. If you lock the front wheel you lose steerage. Avoid skidding.
- Ensure your bike is well set up and

adjusted, if not, downhilling will find the weaknesses.

• Don't fly the humps unless you know what is beyond, and if you're carrying panniers don't fly them at all.

• Select a good line, read the terrain, and hold that line if you are going quickly at all. Altering course at speed can easily induce a slide.

• Try dropping your saddle a couple of inches for long downhills. On very steep downhills it will put you in a more secure position. It helps some people, others simply leave it on its normal setting. Experiment and see what suits you.

• Concentrate, concentrate, concentrate.

The easy way up! In most Alpine resorts bikes can be transported either in cablecars or on the chairlifts. Apart from being tailormade for downhillers facilities like these at Cortina d'Ampezzo, Italy, can seriously extend high-level routes

Don't be frightened to hang out the back. Practise riding above the bike with your arms slightly bent, your bum raised and slightly back, but close enough to drop it down onto the seat again if you should need it. As soon as you approach rough patches get up off the seat a bit, let your arms and legs act as another couple of inches of shock absorbers. If the going becomes extreme, slow right down, virtually to a stop, and hang totally out the back with your stomach on the saddle, just as the trials riders do. You'll find it amazing what you can negotiate in this fashion with real skill.

If you've never tried it, practise on smooth gentle ground and gradually ease into the technical stuff. It might be easier initially just to slide backwards off the saddle rather than rise up then move back.

Ideally you should ride just above the bike at all times when downhilling on single track, it puts you in a position to deal with most unexpected hazards, but it hammers your upper legs, so have a rest on the saddle on the easier bits.

If you do fly, try to keep the bike parallel to the ground, the object is to land both wheels at the same time and start pedalling as soon as possible, this restores total control, then stop pedalling again if necessary. Try and get forwards as you touch down, unless the ground is soft. If the ground is soft move your weight to the rear. Absorb the front wheel impact with your arms and upper body. If the leap is really high stand up quickly and start the landing with your arms and legs virtually straight, it all helps.

Suspension allows you to go faster downhill, it reduces the risk of puncture, and consequently being flung off. There are devotees of all the different types of suspension but for sustained performance and reliability the elastomer based Pace RC-35 fork takes a lot of beating. Much cheaper, if less effective, suspension can be achieved by fitting bigger tyres 2.3inch or even 2.5inch examples now being available.

Safety should always be at the back of your mind. Watch out for obstacles on fast descents, watch out for people, and watch out for animals. That most competent of mountain men Norman Brett lives at the foot of Drummond Hill in Perthshire. He has had so many close calls with deer he has fitted a bell, it saves him whooping constantly on the way down, and

There is more than one school of thought with regard to descending over rough ground. Here Elaine Hopley demonstrates balance, poise, and total control over a really loose section of the Devil's Staircase, one of General Wade's Military Roads in Argyll

Passo di Limo, Dolomiti, North Italy where the occasional passage by rugged four-wheel drive vehicles can make even severely eroded or avalanched hill tracks negotiable again. This is a regular occurrence in many mountainous areas

eliminates the strange looks he used to receive from the two people a year he meets on his nightly training run.

Climbing

Climbing is going to hurt. There will be breathing difficulties, leg aches, and generally feeling awful, even the best guys admit this. Obviously there are different techniques for wide 4WD roads and

technical single track, but broadly the principles remain the same.

Think positive, think this is where you will gain, think beyond the pain beyond the top of the hill, look ahead try to anticipate what's coming up and how you are going to attack it. Some people sing to themselves, they don't have the puff to sing out loud; I try to get a rhythm by counting. You get it wrong but it doesn't matter, keep the rhythm going, keep counting.

Gear selection is paramount. Use a gear you can pedal, not too big, change gear early a little before you need it, that way the change is easy because you don't have full power on. How many times have you seen somebody wait until it's too late to change, weave about the track grinding away as they stand on the pedals, then come to a stop altogether. Change before you need to.

For long steady climbs stay in the saddle, it's more efficient, uses less energy, but for a short steep climb you can do it faster, and probably more successfully, out of the saddle. If it is a really long climb it's a good idea to change position, out of the saddle occasionally to use different muscle groups and stretch.

If the going becomes really steep keep your weight forward to keep the front wheel on the ground, and if this means getting up out of the saddle, do it, but don't lose traction at the rear.

On loose tracks sit back in the saddle for traction before you lose grip altogether, but still maintain the balance of the bike.

Bar ends are good, on a long climb they are really good, you feel as if you can open up your lungs more and use all of your upper body strength. If you are a manual worker your upper body strength will be good, but if you feel you could improve in this department get down the gym and work at it. It will be worth the effort. As usual the fitter you are the better, but it really shows on the climbs.

If you are in a group, don't ride too close, people make mistakes with route choice and with gear changes which can really destroy your rhythm. Make sure you can see the track ahead and ride to suit yourself.

Toeclips help by allowing you to pull up on the pedals as well as press down, SPDs and other clipless pedal

systems are even better because you can pull up more, but if you are forced to dismount do it before you totally run out of steam, it makes the transition from riding to walking, or staggering, that much easier.

Very green and damp underfoot coupled to a long unrelenting climb, Alex Spence demonstrates good gear selection and climbing in the saddle, an effective and efficient style to get him up Langlee Crags, Northumberland

Pushing

When the going becomes so tough you are forced to get off and push the bike remember you'll still need grip, think about a line that will give you room for your feet and room for your bike. A change of sides may be necessary. The non-chainwheel side is better in case the bike slides into you, and you should still be in a

position to apply the brakes whenever you stop or pause.

On exceptionally long pushes consider fastening a rubber bungee from your belt to your rear rack, especially if the bike is heavily

laden. This takes a lot of weight off your arms but of course needs to be allowed for if you are hopping streams or negotiating little bridges.

If the hill is very steep and very rough consider taking off the pedal on the side you are pushing and threading it in from the opposite side. The benefits are twofold: it prevents you barking your shins, and acts as a brake against the downtube when you stop. For total

Getting out of the saddle is often the best way to tackle a short steep climb, provided there is enough grip underfoot

over both shoulders by means of the crossbar and downtube, and across the top of the back using the seat tube. An even more innovative scheme is to balance the crossbar across the top of your rucksack and let the whole thing dangle free.

I use the non-chainwheel side pedal to rest in my midriff and act as a stabiliser. It works but it gets your belly dirty.

It might sound crazy but it is possible to plan a route where the carries always have the bike away from the hillside and consequently less liable to foul anything. Look at the map and try it.

Finally double carries, or even triple carries may be necessary. In big mountain country, it happened to me in the Italian Dolomites, it may be necessary to make more than one journey over a particular stretch. Luggage then bike, for how ever many times it takes. I kept trying to convince myself that I would see more by passing the view twice! It's a bit of a pain, but considerably safer when the occasion demands.

shin safety you could remove the other pedal too and put it in your pocket.

Carrying

Sooner or later on any major route you will resort to carrying. It is never desirable but you can make it tolerable. A purpose made triangular bag like the Trek Shoulder Holder which mounts easily in the main triangle of the frame also doubles as a toolbag as well as providing padding for the shoulder, or you can buy custom tube protection. Personally I use plumber's pipe lagging, it is cheap, sealed cell foam which doesn't absorb water, and you have the choice of several thicknesses.

Some sloping frame designs like the Cannondale make carrying very difficult, and the extra triangles of GT's frames certainly do not help.

Apart from the usual shoulder borne porterage, some folk like to stick their heads right through the main triangle and spread the weight

How to get better at it

Practice makes perfect: the greater the variety of hills that you ride the better. Most mountain bike routes have hills, and the more hills you ride in training the fitter you will be to cope with the tougher routes. Even if you haven't got any big hills, train on what you have, some of the best climbers in recent times have been Dutchmen.

Train by doing repetitions. Choose a hill that takes you two or three minutes maximum to climb. Ride to the top, then slowly back down, recover, then do it again. Repeat the performance four or five times, but don't go until you are ready. The recovery times will gradually decrease, and if possible train with someone who is better than you, but don't go over the top, literally.

Tweaks

These ideas are not really practical when touring, but for one-off attempts on a particular climb they may be possible.

Lighten the bike as much as you can. Take off the panniers, even the rack. Shed the spare bottle and cage, spare tube, virtually all the tools, and mudguards. Travel light yourself, you'll be hot on the way up but take the lightest possible windproof for the descent, or if there's a rifugio at the top buy a paper to stuff down your shirt! If there is you can also dispense with the remaining bottle and cage. Tim Gould even has wheels with fewer spokes for the climbs, but I wouldn't fancy risking them on a rough downhill, and

having toiled up, you are going to enjoy the downhill I hope.

Braking

Ideally all braking should be done in a straight line with the bike upright on a good firm surface, but mountain biking isn't like that. Most of the time, regardless of weather conditions, the surface we ride on is far from firm, and many trails are far from straight, but at least we can aim for perfection.

Try to brake in a straight line, or at the very least do your heavy braking in a straight line and minimise the risk of the bike sliding away from you. Use both brakes, but more back than front, some people achieve this by setting up the front brake with more free play, that way in an emergency the back brake will come on an instant before the front. Unlike riding on the road where most of the braking is done with the front, most of the weight is thrown forwards as you brake, on loose off-road surfaces this could induce a skid. The weight is still thrown forwards as soon as you use the front brake at all, and there are many occasions when you will need all of its power, but try and use the back brake as much as possible without skidding the wheel. Look for firm patches or even bedrock on the trail to kill your speed on big descents,

and when the gradient becomes very severe lean hard on both brakes. The greatest retardation occurs just before lockup. You can achieve this in two ways, either by keeping the brakes on and 'moaning', or by using cadence braking.

Cadence braking is rhythmic braking. As we've just said brakes are at their most effective when on the point of locking up, so it follows that the more frequently you can induce this condition the quicker you should stop. This is the principle behind ABS braking on cars and motorbikes, but you need electronic control to achieve that sort of efficiency. We can at least try by applying the brakes once a second or quicker once you get good at it. It goes without saying that your brakes must be set up correctly with the cables well lubricated.

One of the greatest recent technical innovations are the Mavic ceramic rims. No they are not made of porcelain, the braking surface is impregnated with ceramic 'dust' which produces a surface akin to very fine sandpaper, and improves braking dramatically. Unfortunately the brake-block wear rate increases in proportion.

Erosion is dealt with in depth in Chapter 7, but your improved skills in the braking department will go a long way to help in minimising the effects of your passage.

Gear choice and changing

Most road cyclists pedal at about 90rpm peaking in the region of about 110rpm. While this is an excellent basis for racing on smooth forest roads we must accept that most rides will include many sections where it is most difficult to achieve any rhythm at all, never mind choosing a rhythm we like to pedal.

Different folk have different styles and techniques off-road but wherever possible maintain a good relatively high cadence so your knees don't get hammered by straining too much. Many cycle computers have a cadence mode generated from a sensor mounted on the chainstay which eliminates any guesswork. It is interesting to see how much your intuitive rhythm varies when you check the computer.

Always choose a gear you can pedal without undue strain, especially when hill climbing, it is not automatically the lowest you have available, and there's nothing wrong with standing up on the pedals occasionally to maintain the cadence, or overgearing a short hill with a real attack to surmount it.

Try to keep the chain in a straight line between the front chainrings and the rear block. Effectively this means that only three or four rear sprockets are available for use for any given chainring, but it saves wear and tear and possibly snapping the chain. Such is the multiplicity of mountain bike gears that you will be able to achieve something very close to what you were pedalling before by adjustment of the rear sprockets once you have changed chainrings to keep the chain in line. Avoid extremes.

Change gear in ample time when climbing, this eliminates protracted grinding under load when the hill stiffens. Changing up for downhills isn't so critical but on the descents use as big a chainring as you can. The chain flaps about in the most alarming manner when descending over rough ground, and by increasing the tension by using a big ring you should stop it unshipping.

Well-lubricated cables and mechanisms always work better, especially in wet conditions.

Falling off

You are going to do it, so why not practice. Do it on sand or peat where you are definitely not going to hurt yourself, then move up to some nice grass. Out on the trail, if you do have a choice, try to pick out the best rock free spot! Honest, you do have a choice occasionally!

Chapter 4
Apparel

Mountain bikers ask a lot of their clothing. Ideally it should be warm and comfortable, but not so hot that you melt on the climbs, and sufficiently windproof to prevent chilling on the downhills. Riding bikes, any sort of bikes, over hills and mountains is an exceptionally high-energy sport, obviously you expend an enormous amount of energy and produce prodigious amounts of heat and sweat when climbing at whatever speed you can manage. Then as soon as you crest the col you plummet down the far side creating your own wind chill by the speed you are travelling. This is the reason behind the rather odd sight of Tour riders stuffing newspapers down the fronts of their jerseys at the top of big climbs, and the cause of many riders contracting bronchitis at the height of summer.

Riding a mountain bike up an

Winter trim: seven hours in wet and misty conditions will really test your clothing, and you stand a very good chance of being wet. The important thing now for these riders in Yair, Borders Region Scotland, is to ensure that they stay warm

unsurfaced hill is even more demanding than climbing one of the tarmac Alpine monsters, and it's something a serious mountain biker will do several times a day on the bigger routes, so you very quickly realise the value of good clothing.

Rain is an additional complication. Its effects can be debilitating,

particularly late in the day when you are tired, and there's the added complication that in the mountains it is usually accompanied by wind, which can often be ferocious. In these conditions you need a waterproof, the problem is that unless you use a material that is incredibly breathable you will become just as wet because your sweat cannot escape, or if your outer garment isn't waterproof you will saturate. You would seem to have two choices, either warm and wet or cold and wet, neither being very desirable if you are camping with nowhere to dry your kit at the end of the day.

Don't despair, all is not hopeless, modern materials allow you to build up layers that will wick away moisture from the skin, trap air which warms you up, and protect you from the wind and the rain.

Summer trim: this rider, on the Mount Sinai Summit, Egypt, is well dressed for high terrain in what is usually a hot country

Highland trim! Lochaline, on the Morvern Peninsula is one of the wettest places on mainland Britain, but the locals are well prepared and enjoy their locality regardless

Several manufacturers like Calange, North Cape, Mountain Equipment, Polaris and Karrimor have put a lot of effort into developing garments that get the maximum performance out of these new fabrics, and the results are excellent. There is also a terrific commitment to improving performance both by the fabric manufacturers and the garment makers, so gone are the days of huge bulky waterproofs, not only does today's apparel perform well, it looks good too.

Summer and winter

There is no great separation between summer and winter wear. Your clothing will depend greatly on your environment, the higher you climb the colder it becomes, approximately one degree centigrade for every 150m of height gained, so if your route climbs high be prepared for colder, and possibly wetter, weather and wrap up for those big descents. It is not unusual to see cyclists donning windproof tops at the top of Alpine passes, but expeditioners will tell you to wear everything you possess for some of the 25km downhills in the Andes. Freezing to death could certainly spoil the enjoyment of the downhill!

Helmets

Please wear a helmet, it is worth it. I only used to wear a helmet for racing until I came off so hard on a single track I stuck my sunglasses in the ground. I've worn the bone dome ever since.

It is accepted that climbing on hot days can become more uncomfortable when wearing a helmet, OK so take it off as you climb up the mountain, but put it on again for any downhills. A couple of us were forcing a way out to Ben Alder Cottage on Loch Ericht one boiling July day helmetless, when my colleague came off on a tiny descent and literally stuck his head in a sphagnum bog. The helmet wouldn't have prevented him going in, but would have lessened the depth of sinking. The incident provoked the debate whether or not polystyrene hats would actually be an aid to survival in water. I'll try it when mine's a bit older and declare the results in the reprint!

Helmets work by absorbing and dissipating forces generated in a crash, minimising the effect on your skull. Most modern helmets use expanded polystyrene (EPS) to achieve this. The bubbles sealed within the material deform and break down on impact effectively reducing the amount of shock transmitted to your head. In view of this you should replace your helmet after a serious bump. Some manufacturers like Giro and Specialised recognise this and their warranty facilitates replacement at a reasonable cost.

The EPS body of the helmet will usually have some sort of covering, a thick plastic shell, a thinner lighter microshell or even a lycra mesh. There are pros and cons to each.

The thick plastic shells although undoubtedly very strong can make the helmet heavy and give you neckache at the end of a long day in the saddle. At the other end of the scale the lycra 'softshells' are easily removed for washing and remarkably actually do hold the EPS bodies together after a crash, to the point where you might not discover the helmet fracture unless you remove the cover. Microshells give an excellent compromise between light weight and toughness, and despite their cost have virtually taken over among serious bikers.

Fit

No helmet can be expected to protect you properly if it slops about on your head. Buy one that both fits properly, and looks good. You won't wear it if you think you look daft, so pay a little extra for something that looks good as well as doing the job.

You could well find that your commuting helmet will have you boiling in the hills, make sure you have sufficient ventilation and airflow, you may want to wear it in the Greek Islands or Arizona. On the other hand you would do well to consider running a less ventilated warmer dome in the winter, or choose one where the amount of padding can be reduced to allow the wearing of a thermal hat like a fleece balaclava underneath.

There is no internationally established system for sizing bicycle helmets, the only way is to go and try it on. Most manufacturers rely on three basic shell sizes, small, medium and large, then supply a pack of several thicknesses of padding to fine tune the fit. The system works well because different folk have different shaped heads.

Your helmet should be a snug fit, gripping just enough that rocking it backwards and forwards and side to side should just move your scalp. If you are not happy, try a different padding setup or a different hat. Take your time when buying a helmet, get the shop assistant to help you, it could, or should take a while.

Fitting the helmet

1 The helmet should sit comfortably level on the top of your head, with the front just above your eyes, but clear of your spectacles because it will move about slightly as you ride. Don't tilt it back off your forehead. You should be able to shake

your head about gently without the straps fastened and the helmet stay more or less in place

2 The strap system on most helmets is usually interconnected. One side will have the length preset so adjust the strap on the other side so the intersection is just below the ear too, ensuring that both the front and rear straps are evenly tight. Occasionally the rear strap is a little too loose, adjust to eradicate this. Also ensure that both sets of

side straps settle evenly when tightened. The aim is to get the straps to pull evenly forward and down, and backwards and down to keep the helmet snug on your forehead

3 Adjust the chin strap so that it holds the helmet snugly but firmly on your head. The best way is to adjust the strap too tight, then back it off a little. Properly adjusted the helmet should stay perfectly in place no matter how violently you shake your head

Safety standards

The three main standards to look out for are the American ANSI Z90, or the Snell Foundation B84 and B90, or the British Standard BS6863. There are also the Australian AUS 2063 and the German DIN 33954.

Balaclavas

In extreme winter weather there is a sound case for wearing a balaclava under your crash helmet just as climbers do. Until recently the balaclavas available have been a little

bulky requiring adjustment of the padding in your hat — a bit of a chore in some instances. North Cape have produced a slimline version in Rhovyl, the same stuff as their successful under garments. The balaclava fits without the need for helmet adjustment, but is probably a little light for wearing around camp in the winter.

Shorts

Padded shorts are a must for mountain biking. Even if you are an experienced rider a full day on

bumpy tracks will take its toll. Unlike riding on tarmac roads, the bike is constantly in motion and the place that gets the majority of that movement is your bum.

Synthetic padded inserts have improved considerably in the last few years and are now universally accepted. They wash easily, dry out overnight, and unlike the natural chamois leather originals need no oils or creams to keep them supple enough for re-use. You tend to get what you pay for, so treat yourself, and buy the best you can afford; they'll be well worth it.

Layers

Base layer

To have a successful mountain bike wardrobe you should have: a base layer that will wick away moisture from your skin to keep you dry and warm, a mid layer that will maintain those wicking qualities, presenting the moisture to the air to be dissipated, and providing more warmth and protection from the elements, and lastly an outer or shell layer which is breathable but will shed rain when the occasion arises.

The base layer is the least obvious and the least glamorous but the most important. Until you've experienced the functional luxury of a really good wicking garment you'll have great reservations about spending a lot of money on a thermal top when you can get a cotton T-shirt for much less. Cotton is not satisfactory for winter use, it saturates quite quickly eventually becoming wet and cold, quite the opposite of what is required. On the other hand a good quality polyester blend like Polartec and Capilene will keep you warm and dry. There has recently been a trend towards natural fibres like silk, but these garments require more care in washing and usually don't last as long.

North Cape's Rhovyl Plus gear is competitively priced, very soft to wear, can be hand washed in warm water (40°c), drip-dries quickly and doesn't harbour the bacteria that can make you smell, your travelling companions will appreciate that. It is a little warmer than some of the other items you can get, but their choice of long or short sleeved tops which you can wear as T-shirts, or the long sleeved zipped turtle necks give you something to wear all year round.

Turtle necks are particularly good for winter wear, and if complemented by matching long johns will give you great base layers for the coldest weather. The stretch/recovery qualities of these garments make them ideal for doubling up when it is really bitter and the zipped turtle necks give that extra bit of temperature control on those dreaded uphills.

Warning: read the labels on any thermal garments before tumble drying. You could end up with a ball of sticky polyester.

Mid layer

There is nothing new in the layering system, although modern fabrics have meant it has become wonderfully refined. You can use as

---

Specialist materials

Polartec, Polarlite, Polarsystem and Polarplus are all made by Malden Mills, USA. They are fleeces knitted from 100% Dacron polyester and are used extensively by several garment manufacturers. The material is hard wearing, quick drying, warm and light. Polarlite 1 and 2 have been superseded by Polartec 100 and 200. Polarlite 2 and Polartec 200 are double-sided fleeces. Polartec 300/Polarplus is a heavyweight double-sided fleece for extreme cold weather use. Synchilla is a Patagonia brand name for a Malden fleece.

Charisma derives from Terinda, which is a special type of polyester fibre. It is tightly knitted and then lightly brushed to form a low bulk and wind resistant fleece. Due to its construction it tends to be warmer and more hard wearing than its fluffier counterparts.

Thermalite fleece is knitted fine polyester yarns brushed on its inside surface to create a soft, comfortable stretchy fabric.

Stretchlite, used by Calange for their Stretchlite tights, is a spun polyester with a tough outer surface and soft looped backing. It offers very reasonable wind resistance for a stretch fabric and has a high stretch/recovery ratio.

many layers as the conditions demand, but the principle remains the same, two light layers are much more effective than one great heavy garment, simply because they trap more air.

The equipment appendix to Richard Grant's account of the first ascent of Annapurna 2 in 1960 was written by one Christian Bonnington, and it is worth reflecting on his mid layer, an army shirt, a light and a heavy sweater. Equally remarkable is the appearance of three St Michael sweaters in his personal gear list for the Annapurna South Face expedition in 1970.

Mid layer warmwear is usually manufactured from the more open woven fleeces like Polartec 100 or 200. They are also suitable for outers when you are generating a bit of heat. When choosing a mid layer look for light weight, low pack size, fast drying and lycra cuffs which apart from giving a gentle windseal attract the water and ensure you don't have wet sleeves for long.

North Cape's activity pants and shirts are made of the lighter Polartec 100 which is light and soft and you could wear it next to your skin if you wanted. It dries amazingly quickly, in fact even when totally saturated the kit can be dried in two minutes by whirling it above your head. No doubt any garment made exclusively from Polartec will do the same.

Your fleece might also be needed to keep out the midges even if you are a true Scot! A pestered Elaine Hopley on the Bealach na Lice, Wester Ross in September

Karrimor's Shuna Pullover made from the double sided Polartec 200 is one of the cuddliest garments on the market. It has good elasticated cuffs and hem and is definitely smart enough to wear 'off piste'.

Both of these garments have high collars which are a definite boon first thing on a cold morning, when descending at any time, or when it is wet. This is a design feature found on garments made especially for the more rugged end of the mid layer market, and which border on being all-purpose gear.

Two excellent examples of this are Calange's Ultralite pullover which is neat fitting, has a good

high neck softened with Polartec, an elasticated hem drawcord and lycra bound roll up sleeves in case you get too hot, and the Polaris Forties pullover which has been my constant companion for two years now. When I first saw it I thought it looked a bit on the light side for harsh weather but it has turned out to be excellent. A Pertex lining at the front keeps your chest warm and lycra cuffs drain the water out of your sleeves. When the snow lies on the tops I simply wear two, and if it becomes totally horrendous I use a Polaris Pertex Switchback shell to keep out the worst of the wet.

Outer layer
Ideally an outer, or shell layer should achieve three functions: keep water out, keep heat in, and allow water vapour to escape. This is the area where mountain biking departs from the demands of walkers and climbers, the sustained effort creates tremendous sweat build up that even materials like Sympatex and Goretex cannot cope with it.

There is no doubt that they keep you drier for longer, but is the expense worth it, and do you in fact need total waterproofs?

The answer comes back to the question, where are you going to use the kit, and how often are you going to use it? Some years ago I became convinced that most of my cycling was done in fair weather, but you always remember the soakings. So, for a year I kept an accurate record of the weather between eight and nine in the morning, and five and six in the afternoon, two journeys a day. I was amazed to find it was fair 83% of the time, although on quite a few occasions it was wet underfoot, but only on three journeys during the year did the conditions reach downpour levels. The maximum height of my commuting journey was 112m, and as you climb the incidence of precipitation inevitably rises. Consider however, a much more reliable set of results.

Between 1883 and 1904 records were kept at the observatory on the very summit of Ben Nevis, 1344m, in tandem with recordings in Fort William only seven kilometres away at sea level. On average the temperature on the Ben was 8.6°C colder, it had only two thirds of the sunshine and more than twice the rainfall.

In Britain mountain bike routes seldom reach half the height of Ben Nevis so you can scale down the results accordingly, but if you are frequenting an area of heavy rainfall like the west coast of Scotland, Tierra del Fuego, or Norway, the answer is yes, you do need waterproofs.

One of the best examples of a waterproof jacket designed specifically for the mountain biker is the Thundercloud by Polaris. Featuring two-layer Stowaway Goretex fabric, Pertex and mesh linings, the garment has a storm hood, front pockets, two back pockets with elasticated flap and a 'thru flow' ventilation system – it is really good. The clever cut of the sleeves gives full movement without body rise, and Velcro makes the storm cuffs totally adjustable. Expensive but good value.

Mountain Equipment also have a front runner with their Nimbus jacket which is part of their Compak range, as the name suggests it packs down very small. The fabric is proofed, sanded microfibre, it is light, comfortable and has loads of adjustment using Velcro on the cuffs to really batten down the hatches on megawet days. The front pockets have flaps which are angled forwards and look as if they might let water in, but they don't, in fact they are well sited for bike use. We even turned the Fire Brigade's hose on them to check! The only reservation is the fact that the pockets are at the front, which restricts what you can carry in them on the bike, but this is balanced by the usefulness of the detachable hood which you can wear around camp after you've taken your helmet off.

In an effort to get the best of both worlds some manufacturers have produced reversible jackets, using fleece on one side and Pertex or Tessin on the other. They are rated as windproof and water resistant rather than waterproof, and even then come in various weights.

The Baltoro Windstopper by Karrimor is a real heavyweight, Polartec 200 fleece on one side and Gore Windstopper on the other. This is the sort of kit you would wear if you were going out into the hills in the depths of winter when you shouldn't really be out there at all. It takes a long time to become saturated, but also takes a long time to dry out totally.

North Cape's Reversible Windjac, which is lighter using Polartec 200 and Pertex, is a tried and tested garment which has been around for years. I recall riding in torrential conditions totally saturated, but the Windjac that appeared to be stuck to me was still comfortable.

Lightest of the reversibles and currently the most sophisticated is the Calange Mountainlite which uses Tessin as the windproof section, and microfleece. Developed under extensive field trials it has articulated sleeves so they don't creep up as you ride, a drop tail with a stretch drawcord, underarm zips for extra ventilation and a deep neck zip which aids the built-in air conditioning when you're climbing. A really well-designed garment, with the manufacturers assurance

The tex-es minefield

Tex is a measure of weight in grammes per 1,000 metres of yarn. The remarkable thing about these new generation specialist fabrics listed below is their low tex value. Used on a range of high performance garments their tex is reflected in their super light weight at no cost to the great protection they afford.

What they do and how they work

Goretex is a breathable waterproof fabric. The breathability is down to a microporous membrane made of PTFE (Teflon), which is usually the central element in a three-layer sandwich, although garments where the membrane is the inner of two layer systems are being developed. The outer layer is usually Taslan of varying weights dictated by intended use. The membrane has thousands of tiny pores small enough to let water out but stop rain droplets coming in.

Sympatex has an ultra-thin membrane that is waterproof, windproof and breathable. It works on a molecular scale: water vapour is absorbed and passed along the molecular chains to the outer surface where the water molecules are released and evaporate. The advantage of this process over the porous membrane is that its performance cannot be affected by dirt, salt or cleaning chemicals.

Isofilm is another laminated hydrophilic membrane working on the same principle as Sympatex.

Pertex is a windproof breathable fabric officially rated as showerproof, although the heavier of the six weaves are virtually waterproof. The fabric is produced from microfine yarns and a typical weave has nearly 4000 filaments per square centimetre. Pertex 1000 is a high tenacity ripstop fabric with a hydrophilic coating. The official breathability figures released are 7.5 litres per square metre per 24 hours, which is probably currently the best available for any material.

CoSal 21 is also polyester microfine yarns woven tightly together, similar to Pertex.

H2NO is a Patagonia branded coating, very waterproof and supple, perhaps not as breathable as some.

Entrant, Millair, Hydro-dry, Technique XP, are all coatings either hydrophilic or microporous which are applied to various fabrics. Coated fabrics are usually cheaper than the laminates, don't perform quite as well, but often represent good value for money.

PU Nylon and Neoprene are totally waterproof but don't breathe at all. Cheapest around and fine in an emergency. Some of the coatings flake off if stuffed into a bag regularly and then all you are left with is a nylon jacket. Never wash them.

that it can be reproofed with Nikwax or the like when its water repellent qualities fade.

Legs

Keeping your legs warm isn't as critical as your torso, and you see folk persevering with shorts in the most inclement of weather. But there is no denying that your legs function better when they are warm and you are less likely to cause muscle damage.

As long as you have a good pair of padded shorts you can wear just about anything over the top. However, the colder the weather the more desirable good bottoms become, particularly when the tracks are covered with water. Cheaper bottoms deform when wet and if the seat loses its shape getting back onto the saddle can become a problem. Pulling your own trousers down on the nose of the saddle can be as awkward as it is embarrassing.

Bib style or salopettes are the most satisfactory for cold conditions as they eliminate all risk of a gap at the back. Good conventional thermal bib tights are excellent, but so too are some makes of fleece salopettes for climbers. They dry out much quicker than the thermal bibs. The legs of some are too wide at the bottom and catch in the chainrings, but North Cape's Polartec

Salopettes have elasticated ankles, three zipped pockets, zipped fly and reinforced seat and knee, and are excellent. I have used these for the last two winters, and while you don't want too much in your pockets in case you come off the bike, they are handy, and the zipped fly is a positive boon in cold weather.

Other options for the legs are Stretchlites by Calange and the ever faithful Ron Hill Tracksters which now come in two weights. A lot of purists level criticism at lightweight bottoms, but look how many people wear them in the hills, surely another pointer to the fact that the high-level mountain biker is closer to the fell runner, the cross-country skier and the mountaineer than the road cyclist.

Hands

You must have padding for your hands for mountain biking, and even then big days in big hills can cause numbness. It is not unknown for handlebar grips to deform on long Alpine descents, so imagine what sort of punishment your hands are taking.

Good leather trackmitts still seem

Gloves: Ozzo leather palmed thermal training gloves (Top) North Cape thermal Gripper gloves with rubberised palms (Centre) Karrimor Polartec lined Windstopper gloves (Bottom)

to be the best, although Bob Simpson's gradually disintegrated as he rode across Australia due to a liberal daily dose of sweat and overnight drying out, but that was a bit extreme. Many of the gel padded mitts become useless when the gel gets squeezed to the edges of the palm compartment, and apart from not doing its job in the central area, it becomes uncomfortable elsewhere.

In winter wear light thermal gloves under your mitts, or thick thermal training gloves over them. The best so far are OZZO which have soft white leather palms with wear area reinforcements, a thermal lining and a breathable fabric back. Mountain biking in the wet really hammers gloves as I found when my beautiful Duegis disintegrated on the Polaris Challenge and I had to resort to a pair of ex-RAF woollies, which worked very well. Days aren't so long in the winter so you can get away with less padding.

Footwear

The ideal all-round mountain bike footwear hasn't been designed yet, and most people end up with two or three pairs of shoes or boots to suit different aspects of the sport. People use everything from trainers to stout walking boots.

The type of terrain to be traversed dictates what is best suited, but if you've got a favourite pair of anything you'll tend to use them. With the much wider acceptance of toeclips the stouter boots are fading

from the scene, but as long as they are slim enough in the toecap and don't interfere with your pedalling action they are still worthy of consideration for the rougher, higher, longer routes when there will be a lot of enforced walking.

Another major factor is how fit and how technically competent you are, which will also dictate how much walking you do.

One of the main considerations should be the shoe's waterproof qualities which has been totally disregarded by virtually all mountain bike shoe manufacturers with the result that the serious cross-country travellers still use walking footwear of one sort or another. In this department the Goretex Karrimor KSBs are excellent. They don't restrict pedalling and are as waterproof as they claim. Lightweight trekking shoes tend to be more suitable for very hot countries.

The shoes compatible with Shimano's SPD clipless pedals and similar designs have one disadvantage. The cleat area, which coincides with the ball of the foot, and area of greatest purchase, is of

Waterproof Karrimor Goretex KSBs will fit in toeclips if the straps are backed off. The addition of gaiters will provide waterproof protection up to the knees

necessity manufactured of hard material which is quite lethal on wet rock when you are forced to walk. This was amply demonstrated to me one day when making a crossing of the Bealach na Lice, Wester Ross, with former Scottish mountain bike champion Elaine Hopley, who can outpedal me any day of the week. There is a section above Loch Coire Fionnaraich where the track crosses a great slab of bedrock. It was quite wet, mossy, and angled. As I approached I saw Elaine, who was quite some distance ahead of me, working her way up the side having deemed it safer to avoid the slab in her SPDs, whereas I had no difficulty walking across in my Duegi GG cyclo-cross shoes even with the studs. However, the advantage was short lived, she blew me off in a major way on the final climb to the col.

Comfort and fit

Feet come in many different shapes and sizes, and it is not unusual to have one foot slightly larger than the other. The main thing involved is the 'last' or base of the shoe, and if you have broad feet Italian footwear might be too narrow. Sizing is not consistent so it is absolutely essential to try shoes on with the socks you intend to wear in the hills.

Stiff soled shoes, aimed at transmitting all your power to the pedals when racing, are far from ideal when walking, and for extended tours you must go for comfort, and versatility because they may be the only footwear you have with you.

For winter or colder riding, there is no point in cramming two pairs of socks and your feet into your normal shoes. This will restrict the circulation of the blood to such a degree that your feet will freeze quicker than ever.

Some of the best socks currently available are Thorlo which are soft, durable and have excellent thermal qualities. In summer conditions you can go as light as you want, but in winter think more as a mountaineer than a cyclist.

The last element of comfort is ease of access to the toeclips or speed of cleat location. Sole pattern can greatly affect the ease of entry to the toeclips and overall efficiency.

There is nothing more frustrating than fiddling about trying to get an awkward shoe into a toeclip, especially when the restart is slightly uphill. If at all possible choose a shoe that has a backwards facing sole pattern, and is devoid of lateral straps across the front. This of course does not apply to SPDs.

Gaiters

In very wet conditions underfoot, like the British winter (and even many summers too!) the lower legs and feet can be well protected by gaiters. The cheapest are invariably best suited because they are more flexible, but still tend to catch the cranks on every pedal stroke. This can either drive you mad, or be very reassuring depending on your point of view. However, the cheapest solution to dry feet is to cover your socks with plastic bags before putting your boots on. Not pretty, but effective!

Eyewear

Glasses or shades are essential. They keep out insects, wind and dust in the summer, and snow, mud and crud in the winter. They protect you from stray branches when weaving through trees, and shades are a most important factor in preventing snow blindness and the sun's glare.

Clear lenses allow you to appreciate all the natural colours of the countryside, so special in the hills late in the day, yellow or orange lenses have the advantage of boosting contrast in overcast daylight, while reflective coatings have the advantage of reducing glare and looking incredibly trendy, which might or might not appeal to you. They are intended for use in very bright conditions and are especially good in sunlit snow, however, they need careful handling since the coatings are not scratchproof and must be stored in their case and only cleaned with the proper lens cloth.

Some glasses come with adjustable earpieces, if they don't make sure they can be bent to ensure a snug fit. One or two have a tilt adjustment to tuck them down onto your cheek, a major factor in keeping out the mud thrown up off your front wheel.

The more expensive models, and some of them are really expensive, invariably come with two or even three interchangeable lenses, but it's more important to check that they are designed to resist impact, usually achieved by using a polycarbonate often disguised under a trade name.

Chapter 5
Fitness and pacing

This chapter is not intended as a training manual, specialist guidance of that nature has been the subject of whole books themselves, but after your first day in the hills you will have realised that the fitter you are, the more enjoyable your mountain biking will be. One of the best books giving guidance on training programmes is *Mountain bike racing* by Tim Gould and Simon Burney. (See Bibliography)

Goal setting

What do you want to be able to achieve? Either in the way of overall fitness, or in the ability to cover long distances over difficult terrain. You won't increase your fitness overnight, it will take months, and at times you will wonder whether you are actually making any progress at all. The only real way to reassure yourself is to keep a record of your efforts. Probably the simplest, and it worked for me, is to record the time taken to cycle to work. Soon after you start, on the days when making the effort is hard, or you don't want to hurt or put up with the distress of the ride, you'll realise you must have a goal to sustain the effort to maintain the discipline. If you are racing mountain bikes it might be relatively easy, you can aim for a top 10 or top 20 placing, and it might not be a bad idea to do a few races simply for this reason. Your other goal should be to complete a day out in the hills, or an expedition, without serious distress, it **is** supposed to be enjoyment after all. Set a goal which is not out of reach, but which is a serious challenge. To make significant improvements you need a structured training regime.

Limitations

If you are in full-time employment the greatest limitation is time available for training. Those who are unemployed can structure their training programme, and many have done, to such a degree that one member of the Hades 69 club suggested there should now be two sub classes within the accepted race classifications: Working and Unemployed.

A good way to maximise your time is to cycle to work. The most successful season, both in race results and in leisure riding, I ever had was when I unfailingly rode to work every day, two stints of 11 miles, and the money I saved in petrol paid for my race entry fees.

There are disadvantages, you put yourself at risk when riding in frost or darkness. I overcame the former by using the mountain bike, but the salted roads really hammered the alloy if I didn't wash it off after each journey; and the latter by devising extra high-visibility clothing and accessories for the darkness. I even went as far as having a pair of double thickness white tights made, which forced me to sneak out of work like a fugitive from the corps

One of the smoothest routes in rough countryside. All members of the team enjoying the pace. Elgol, Isle of Skye, February

de ballet, but they worked, I never got knocked off, and made a whole new circle of friends!

We aren't all superhumans, the sad fact is most of us are not. Don't expect to become as good as someone who is a natural athlete, and who also trains methodically, so we're never going to be that good, but undoubtedly with application and effort we can all improve, and make mountain biking more enjoyable for ourselves.

Training

Never slavishly copy anyone else's training routine. Inevitably those published are those used by successful riders, but they have probably developed them over a period of years, and started their current system from a far more established base than the average rider.

If you are new to the sport the best basis to start from is that of endurance. Ride your road bike or buy a pair of slicks for your mountain bike and try to do two or three hours on the road, two or three times a week. The reason for riding the road as opposed to the hills, which is what you really want to do, is that initially a constant steady pace will build up your stamina, which cannot be achieved in the hills. You are either right on the limit trying to conquer a climb, freewheeling down a tricky descent, or even walking, none of these are any good for initial fitness.

If you haven't been on a bike for years, or perhaps never at all,

The best aid to training is a cycle computer, everyone wants to know how long they have been out and how far they have gone. Better still if you buy one with a cadence mode

A basic programme

Ideally all your riding should be done at 80rpm or more, if you can achieve this you will reduce the risk of knee problems through straining in too high a gear, maintain flexibility, and gear changing will become second nature. This is the reason for buying a computer with a cadence mode if you can afford it. Obviously when you first start, you cannot ride up hills at these revolutions so choose a flat course. If it becomes windy change down the gears to keep the revs up, you are not too concerned with the distance covered. The goal is 1,000 miles of riding, mainly on the flat. A suggested programme is as follows:

First 10 days
Set out on your flat road course by either looking at your watch or starting your computer. Aim to ride at 80rpm and pedal all the time, no freewheeling. Ride for exactly 15 minutes, turn around and ride back. Watch your time, it might take you 16 minutes to ride back. This first 10 days need not be consecutive but you'll get fitter quicker if they are. You'll probably have ridden about eight miles, and by the time you get showered it will have taken you about an hour altogether.

If you've ridden your 30 minutes for five days that will have produced 40 miles. An enjoyable day out covering perhaps 15 miles in the

How far are you going? How long will it take? Glen Applecross, Wester Ross, Scotland is a serious commitment in itself, the route disappears over the cloud covered ridge in the far distance. It is likely that it will also include only one leg of a long route in wild country. Good pacing will be essential for a successful completion

consider a medical check up before you start. Just go out for an hour, no more, once a week for four weeks, but don't miss, and don't kill yourself. Then ride at a comfortable pace twice a week for four weeks. Build up slowly.

to measure your pedal revolutions, then when you really get into it you can either buy or borrow a heart monitor to analyse your performance. Beware, training can take over your life to the point where it becomes an end in itself.

hills will bring your total to 55 miles for the week, so by the time you go into the second phase of the 10 days you'll have clocked 110 miles.

Second 10 days
Up your flat riding to 30 minutes out and back, same 80rpm, and repeat this each day. You'll do roughly 16 miles each session, so your weekly total will climb to 95 with a similar day out in the hills at the weekend, and by the end of the month you'll have 300 miles under your belt. Still mainly road work.

Third 10 days
By now you will be well at home with your bike and will be able to bring some serious FLAT miles into your programme. Alternate easy rides, 20 miles or less, with long rides, 20 miles and more, and attempt to do a good long ride of 35 to 40 miles once a week. You'll now eat into that goal of 1,000 flat miles at a cracking rate and no doubt you'll get into the way of road training once or twice a week as a way of life. A good idea is to put the knobblies on for the weekend, and ride the slicks during the week.

Steps to further improving performance
You now get into the realms of cardiac related serious training and the need for professional advice. It's a new world of lactate profiles, maximum heart rates, and training

levels. If you are going to become this serious contact one or more of the following: British Mountain Bike Federation 0536 412211, the BMBF will put you in touch with a local training coach; Crewe and Alsager College 0270 8781721 (speak to the Sport & Exercise Research and Development Unit, it will cost you, but you'll find out a whole lot you never knew about yourself); Wheel Fitness (Coaching) 0782 21235.

Stretching

Stretching keeps the muscles supple, prepares you for movement, and helps you make the transition from inactivity to vigorous activity without undue strain. It is especially important if you cycle because this is an activity that will promote tightness and inflexibility in certain areas. Stretching before and after you ride will keep you flexible and go some way towards preventing muscle injuries. Stretching is easy, and should be kept so, but if it is done incorrectly it can do more harm than good. For this reason it is essential to understand the right techniques so seek the advice of a physiotherapist, coach or trainer, or consult an authoritative manual such as *Stretching* by Bob Anderson. (See Bibliography)

When done correctly it feels

good. You don't have to push the limits or attempt to go further every day; it's not a competition. Your stretching routine should be tailored to your own particular muscle structure, flexibility and tension levels. The key is regularity and relaxation. The object is to reduce muscular tension thereby promoting freer movement. It is well worth a few minutes every day.

Pacing

How far are you going? How long have you to do it?

Pacing isn't so critical on short days, four hours or less on the bike. You can live off your reserves for this sort of time in most conditions, some riders hardly eat to top up their energy levels for this sort of ride. You can go quicker simply because you'll not be doing it for so long, but on arduous going it will still pay to keep a bit in reserve in case of accident.

Long days are a different proposition. The way you treat them will depend on your level of fitness, what you are used to doing, and what your goal is at the end of the day. It is essential to have a good energy intake, and appropriate rests. We all vary in our food and rest requirements and there are different approaches. I offer the following merely as suggestions that worked in certain situations. They may work for you too, but as always, can be adapted to the conditions of the day, weather, terrain, and how you actually feel.

Polaris System: The Polaris Challenge is a two day event. A first day of seven hours riding, the second limited to five hours. Most folk stoke live on Maxim, but it's nice to have something to chew. Dried fruit or nuts and raisins are good, and don't forget the liquid.

Most Polaris competitors aim to do about 10 miles per hour, which is fast, but there's often the option of tarmac which can boost your average

The Wetland Way, sorry Southern Upland Way approach: a different aim here, 220 miles in five days, over some really testing terrain, 82% off-road. The weather was diabolical most of the way, anyone with a ha'porth of sense would have abandoned! The basic difference was that the effort had to be sustained for five days, as opposed to one and a half. Day one was 10 hours, day two was 11 hours, day three also 11 hours, day four was 10 hours, and day five a measly six hours. The average daily mileage was about 45.

Adrian Gidney and Glenn Wilks nibbled Mars bars, Fruesli bars, nuts and raisins, and Bombay mix as they rode, but had tea stops dictated both by terrain and availability. A typical day went as follows:

Make use of any available cover or protection for breaks, especially in windy conditions. Stells (Northumbrian sheepfolds) make excellent venues

up with pasta the night before, and have a high energy breakfast too. The idea is to keep going for as much as possible of the seven hours, that way you'll probably cover more miles and score more points. It is so easy to forget to eat on the trail, just as easy when touring as in competition, if you feel a bit light headed your blood sugar level is usually going down, so get some food immediately. You can considerably. A totally off-road situation could well halve this. The average is maintained by eating on the move or nibbling at enforced stops for map reading. Little and often, keep the food intake going. Another aid to pacing is sharing the lead, teams of two on the Polaris. This tends to keep the pace even and staves off fatigue. You don't need to think so much when you're following!

0720hrs	Rise. Breakfast, porridge with honey, rolls and marmalade, tea
0918	Start
1130	Coffee from flask, fruit cake. 5 minutes rest
1210	Proper brew, cuppasoup, tea, fruit cake 25 minutes rest
1410	Brew, tea, meat pie, oranges 30 minutes rest
1700	Brew, tea, cake 20 minutes rest
2020hrs	Finish in darkness. Pasta dinner, rice pudding, tea. Dry out kit!

Long summer days can be used to make your journeys more relaxing. You can afford to take more time, it's not going to get dark at seven o' clock, just go out and enjoy the day. Switch off and spend more time drinking in your surroundings than dripping sweat. It is an individual choice.

In good conditions, enforced breaks caused by punctures can be used as recovery periods by those not involved in the repairs, but if the weather is bad or the breakdown occurs in an exposed situation, everyone should lend a hand to minimise the risk of exposure due to rapid cooling

Estimating time

People always ask 'How far have you been today?' Mountain biking, unlike road cycling, must take into consideration the full spectrum of road and track surfaces, or even lack of them. It is a much fairer reflection to talk in terms of how many hours effort you put into a day. Estimating

distances is dealt with in Chapter 7 Navigation.

Let us look at a 12-mile loop. If it is entirely on well-surfaced forest road it would probably take less than an hour to complete. If in the forest, but using less frequented roads which have become mossy and overgrown through lack of use, it would take a full hour at least. These tracks would be marked on the OS map as 'white' roads bordered by pecked lines. Now consider a similar white road traversing open moorland. It could be a good landrover track or grousemoor road, or a virtually disused unclassified county road, similar timings might apply, but some old unclassified roads have deteriorated to such an extent that they barely exist on the ground and you might take nearly two hours for your loop.

A very rough guide can be, smooth tracks to buildings, rough tracks to pastures. The buildings will

be marked on the OS map. A 'white' going to a building might well have been maintained to some degree because the building is still in use, no matter how remote, it may even be an occupied house. On the other hand a road simply terminating at the edge of a moor and becoming a bridleway in all probability will only be used by large agricultural machinery which isn't averse to a rut or two. No doubt the very first time you'll apply this in unknown territory I'll be proved wrong! Sorry.

Of course if your chosen 12-mile route lies entirely over a red dashed bridleway it could take a full four hours!

Terrain

Assessment

Another rough guide to the time you'll take is to multiply your normal time taken to cover the same distance on the road: by two as soon as you ride off-road at all, farm tracks, old county roads, forestry, by three for any lengths of single track and walking, I know you'll be quick downhill, but the uphills can be pretty slow if you're forced to plod, and by four for any sections where carrying is involved. They are usually very short, apart from some of the Alpine or Himalayan horrors, but absorb a lot of time.

Mark the times on your map as you travel along any given route and work out the relevant times for a particular terrain when you get home. Within a few months you'll have covered most types of terrain and become quite expert at estimation. You'll also have realised the difference between what is marked on the map and what actually exists on the ground.

Relating speed to terrain

The main factor apart from the condition of the terrain itself affecting your progress will be the gradient. It even alters the terrain itself. What can be a fairly well-surfaced mountain track can deteriorate enormously in the steeper sections due to water erosion, to the point where, high in the Dolomites especially, you find concreted hairpin bends after many kilometres of loose surfaced climbing. One I encountered in the Valle di Fanes on the way to the Passo di Limo claimed to be 36%, and I believed it. My attempt at riding failed miserably and even walking up the concrete on my toes was difficult. It must be a good vehicle that ferries supplies to the rifugio at the top.

Most maps have the contours marked and you can see at a glance how steep the tracks are by the density of the brown lines. Bear in mind the scale of the map you are using and the contour gap: is it 5m, 10m, or even 20m? I got a nasty shock the first time I went to the Alps with the bike. I bought an excellent 1:25,000 map, noticed that there were a lot of contours, that's why I went, but couldn't understand why I was walking all the time. The lines didn't seem that close together, but I had been using 1:50,000 Landrangers at home, on this map the same density of contour lines meant twice as steep.

Maps that don't have the contours marked, usually 1:200,000 and smaller, supplement the information with generous helpings of spot heights, so at least you'll know the height of the pass you are aiming for, but you could get a shock or two on the way. Use the small-scale maps for overall planning and buy a 1:50,000 or larger when you get there.

Changes in the terrain itself

I am tempted to say that extremes in weather can affect some types of terrain to the point where your estimated speed over them will be way out from the norm. But what is the norm?

Hard surfaces aren't affected too much, but the star example must be peaty tracks. If we accept the norm as wet squelchy going, not really suited to cycling at all, variations either side of this can cut minutes or even hours off your times. At the height of a very dry summer the peat moors dry out to such a degree that you're frightened to use your stove in case you set them alight. In this state the tracks dry out superbly and the passage of our pedestrian brethren smoothes out the surface to such a degree that riding is possible, and usually very enjoyable. At other times a desperate carry has been the order of the day, unless it is mid winter when these same tracks can freeze solid due to their high water content, and again become negotiable. The answer for peaty tracks would appear to be mid-summer, or mid-winter.

Stony tracks are often at their worst at Easter time, just after the snows have melted, at the end of the worst of the wet-winter season. They improve considerably with the passage of feet or wheels and can be a much quicker ride by the end of the summer. It's not just the sunshine that makes summer times better than the grey days of winter. Think about the terrain you are about to cover. Has there been any recent rain? How will it have affected the surfaces? Might it be better to avoid this area for a couple of weeks to let it dry out? There are some places not worth visiting during wet spells because they are so difficult, and there is also the erosion factor to consider.

Breaks

In most cases the terrain will dictate when you take a break. If the climbing is gradual five or 10 minutes every hour might be acceptable, but if the terrain is steep from the outset it might be advisable to take five minutes every half hour. Do **not** wait until exhaustion threatens before you take a break. Fit your riding pattern to the ability of the weakest member of the party, they probably won't tell you they are knackered, so keep a close eye on them and give them a chance. In good conditions enforced breaks caused by punctures or other mechanical maladies can be used as recovery periods for those not involved with the repairs, but if the weather is bad or the breakdown occurs in an exposed situation, everyone should lend a hand to minimise the risk of exposure due to rapid cooling. See if you can find a more sheltered spot by walking a short distance. This is especially important in winter.

Choose the site for any break carefully, make maximum use of any natural cover: walls and dense hedges can be good, stells (sheepfolds) even better. Get out of the wind any way you can, even simply lying in a hollow can help enormously, but choose a dry one!

As soon as you stop don your windproof, sit on something waterproof, some bumbags like the MacPac Marathon have built-in mini foam mats for this purpose. And keep an eye on the weather.

Modified Naismith's rule

Analysis of the time taken to cover routes in mountainous terrain is not an exact science due to variable factors like the weather, the ground etc, but for many years walkers and mountaineers have used Naismith's rule as a rough guide when planning the timing of routes. This is 3mph plus half an hour per 1,000 feet of climbing, transposed to a metric equivalent of 5kph plus half an hour per 300 metres of climbing. I have chosen the metric version for this example because of the fact that the grid on an OS map is kilometre squares and easy to estimate without instrumental measurement.

On most terrain a mountain biker will climb only slightly faster than a walker, say 7kph, but on the descents 15kph can be averaged, or even well exceeded. So timing predictions can be more complicated, and you should consider the type of track and its contours. Reasonably accurate estimations will only be achieved by monitoring your own performance on a number of routes, but you can achieve a rough estimate as below.

Example:
Route 30km total, 15km out and back, rising 600m

Outward uphill leg $\dfrac{15\ km}{7kph} \quad + \quad \dfrac{600m}{300} \quad x \quad 0.5hr$

$\quad = \quad 2.4 \quad + \quad 1 \quad = \quad 3.14\ hrs$

Downhill homeward leg $\quad \dfrac{15\ km}{15\ kph} \quad = \quad 1\ hr$

Estimated total time (uphill plus downhill) 4.14 hrs or four hours eight minutes. Very few routes are as straight forward as this, but there are some occasions when it is necessary to be as accurate as possible, and this may help.

Chapter 6
Where to ride

Rights of way

People have been taking bikes over the hills for years. The earliest British description I have come across appeared in *Cycling* (now *Cycling Weekly*) on 18 May 1919, and concerned a crossing of the Berwyn Mountains near Cynwyd in snowy conditions. No one minded where you were in those days, they simply looked at you askance and passed quietly by, but the mountain bike has changed all that. This amazing leap forward in bicycle design has meant that you can actually now ride off-road instead of carrying or wheeling, which was 95% of pass storming as the old diehards still call it, and as a result there are more of us doing it. Only natural. Unfortunately there is some overcrowding in the honeypot areas and occasional clashes of interest. Mountain bikers are the new boys on the block and attract most of the blame, rightly or wrongly.

There is now a need for newcomers to the sport to be advised where we can and cannot ride, and perhaps remind some of the elders of the situation on rights of way. I am sure there is plenty of room for us all if we spread out. It will also help a lot if you are sure you are riding legally when challenged by some snotty walker.

Categories of rights of way

England and Wales
A footpath is a right of way on foot, nothing else. Keep off them on your bike **unless** you have the landowner's permission. Even motor vehicles can be given permission to use footpaths, it happens all the time on grouse moors and where vehicles require access to reservoirs and radio masts. Some footpaths have had roads superimposed upon them by landowners and tenants, as they are perfectly entitled to do, but many other splendid old roads were awarded only footpath status when the definitive parish maps were prepared in the 1950s. One such track is the Holdenhurth Band in Upper Teesdale near Cow Green Reservoir: it is an old mine road, possibly even the original road through the valley into Cumbria. Now beautifully grassed over it is firm, well drained, and well defined, but still only officially a footpath. Tragic. A star example of a situation where it is physically quite easy to ride but legally prohibited.

A bridleway is a right of way on foot and on horse, and extended to include bicycles by Section 30 of the Countryside Act 1968 which states, 'Any member of the public shall have, as a right of way, the right to ride a bicycle, not being a motor vehicle, on any bridleway, but in exercising that right cyclists shall give way to pedestrians and persons on horseback. It is perfectly legal to ride on bridleways.

A *byway* (The full title is Byway Open to All Traffic) is, as the name implies, open to anything including motor vehicles - unless specific restrictions, usually pertaining to motor vehicles, have been imposed by a Traffic Regulation Order. Up until now most of the byways subject to restriction have been old unpaved routes that were badly damaged by four-wheel drive vehicles, and it is they that have been restricted.

A road used as a public path is the greatest source of confusion in the entire rights of way sector. The Countryside Act 1968 recognised this and directed that every road used as public path should be reclassified as either a 'Byway open to all traffic', a 'Bridleway' or a 'Footpath'. However they still appear on maps probably due to the time that it takes to review them and the fact that the subsequent Wildlife and Countryside Act 1981 directed that the reviews be carried out 'as soon as reasonably practicable', which could be any time. Eventually they will disappear but in the meantime cyclists are probably safe to use them because most do carry evidence of vehicular rights.

Unclassified county roads are mostly byways, but those that interest us are the unsurfaced variety. Definitely the most difficult to discern from the OS map. The only certain way

Bridleway, High Street, Cumbria. This tiny little track is what remains of the old Roman Road which runs from Troutbeck to Askham along the high ridge. It has been accorded bridleway status

More and more unclassified roads are being marked with the distinctive 'Byway Open to All Traffic' symbol on OS Landranger maps, but many still remain purely as 'white' roads. This example, near Morpeth, Northumberland, has all the looks of a private estate road

The only clue to the existence of an unclassified road often lies in the 'Unsuitable For Motors' signpost. The tracks themselves are often mere depressions across a grassy meadow

Below: a typical unclassified road, stony base, many gates mainly used by agricultural traffic, but excellent for mountain bikes. Near Roddam Rigg, Northumberland

is to take your own map along to the County Council Rights of Way or Highways department and transfer the details from their definitive maps. Unclassified roads can be drawn on OS maps as 'white' roads or even a black dashed line or may not even appear at all which is a bit naughty. The only clue possibly being a signpost declaring 'Not Suitable For Motors', irresistible! Some guidebooks (like mine!) include a selection researched by the authors, so by using them you'll get an idea of what to look for.

Having said all of this it must be emphasised that these are the legal definitions and in no way reflect the quality of the trail. You can see this from the photographs. You get motorways like the Pen-y-ghent track which is only a footpath, bridleways that vary from the road up Mickleden in the Lake District to a line of boardwalks along the Border Ridge in the Cheviot Hills, or the squelchy path that is the Lakeland High Street in places. You see unclassified roads that are a mere depression across a field or an overgrown lane where you really need your eyewear to eliminate risk of damage to your sight. The only true test is to ride them.

Scotland

In Scots Law there is no hard and fast classification of different types of rights of way. It is usual, however, to distinguish between rights of way on foot, on horseback, or in carts or carriages. In Scotland, as distinct from England, the greater of these rights, ie motor vehicles, include the lesser, ie horses, bicycles and pedestrians, so that proof of a right to use the route for vehicular traffic would include the various lesser rights.

Alas readily available maps do not differentiate and guide the user with the category of track, in fact the OS maps have two disclaimers. One, at the beginning of the 'Roads and Paths' key saying 'Not necessarily rights of way', and the other at the end of the Public Rights of Way section saying 'Not Applicable to Scotland'. They are fireproof, but

acquiescence of the landowner and there have been remarkably few disputes. Most landowners are pleased to permit access, providing damage and disturbance are not caused and that the public act in a responsible manner.

However, should you diverge from a right of way or follow a route which is not a right of way, you should have regard for the interests of the occupier of the land. This is especially true in the lambing season, the grouse shooting and deer stalking seasons.

The physical appearance of a track on the ground often bears little relation to its official status. This 'motorway' on Pen-y-ghent, West Yorkshire, bears only Footpath status, but has been especially reinforced and surfaced to limit the amount of damage and erosion caused by foot passengers

Unfortunately it is not wholly clear whether a right of way for pedestrians includes a right of way by bicycle, but it is generally accepted that it does.

how are we to know what is what?

The obvious answer is we don't. The practise in Scotland has for many years been that the public have been permitted access to the land with the

General right of way requirements

The general requirements and guidelines for a Scottish Right of Way can be defined as follows, subject to one or two technical qualifications.

1 The track must run from one public place to another public place
2 The track must follow a more or less defined route
3 For a right of way to be created, the track must have been used openly and peaceably by members of the public without the permission, express or implied, of the landowners
4 It must have been so used without substantial and effective interruption for a period of 20 years or more

Seasonal considerations

Lambing: the exact time of lambing in Scotland (and England too) varies according to the area, the higher or the further north you go the later it will be, but generally it is between mid-April and the end of May. **Red deer stalking**: the open season for culling red deer stags is from 1 July–20 October, and for hinds from 21 October–15 February. However, the most important time is generally from mid-August to mid-October.

It is well worth contacting the stalkers for any area you intend to visit, not only will this eliminate any conflict of interests, but their local knowledge can be worth its weight in gold. You will find their details and telephone numbers in *Heading For The Scottish Hills* listed in the Bibliography. **Grouse shooting**: the grouse shooting season runs from 12 August–10 December, with most action during the earlier part of that period. **Birds nesting**: all ground nesting birds on moorland are very vulnerable to disturbance, so take particular care at nesting time.

From this it can be seen that use by pedal cyclists of a road or track for the prescriptive period described above would no doubt create for cyclists a right of way over that road or track, so we could be considerably indebted to the old pass stormers and rough stuffers who have been dragging their steeds all over the Highlands for years.

A public right of way can only be constituted by members of the public 'possessing' the route, in the sense of actually passing over it with a fair degree of regularity. The amount of use is an individual matter; in a thinly populated area, less use would be required than in a densely populated district. In a case

fought by the Scottish Rights of Way Society in 1887 the fact that there was little or no evidence of use during the winter months of the road from Clova to Braemar Glen Doll did not prevent the Court holding that there was a public right of way.

In all fairness the vast majority of routes that mountain bikers will wish to ride will be well-trodden tracks because the lesser paths are so rough they are unridable, so there should be few problems.

Extinction of rights of way

Just as rights of way can be created by regular use over the 20-year period, so can they be lost if they

are not used. This makes it vitally important, particularly on the less frequented routes, to exercise your right of passage. Even historically important routes, such as parts of the roads built by General Wade or William Caulfield, could cease to be rights of way because they are not too attractive to walkers, but some are great for mountain biking. Keep a diary of your journeys, you never know when it might become vital evidence.

Voluntary restrictions

Despite the remoteness of much of Scotland virtually all of it is someone's working environment. Regardless of your personal views on income being derived from the likes of grouse shooting or deer stalking, we must accept responsibility for our behaviour, and respect to the full the requirements of the estates for a small part of the year, mid-August to mid-October. If possible keep off the hill for this period, or at the very least check with the stalker or the estate office. In this way we should continue to enjoy the amazing Scottish landscape.

North America

Every State has its own restrictions. The only way to ride legally is to make contact with the State Park Office and find out for yourself. Like anywhere different conditions

Changes in terrain: this direction is OK, the route turns from steep downhill grassy single track into stony farm road then onto tarmac in four hundred metres, but the opposite direction is a bit of a shock, especially in winter when the sunken single track frequently has icy stretches

prevail at different times of year, and what may be safe or environmentally acceptable during one season may be banned at another. The definition of 'wilderness' seems to have local interpretations too, in Arizona it is officially off limits to all vehicles beyond the wilderness line, but most terrain leading up to it is National Forest and they don't mind bicycles, but in Colorado the wilderness areas are closed to cyclists, so it is imperative that you check locally.

Most trails and dirt roads are used by a variety of recreationists, hikers, horse riders, motorcyclists, four-wheel drive enthusiasts and of course mountain bikers. It is only reasonable to be polite and considerate when riding.

Getting around the rules

The official rights of way aren't the only places you can ride. More and more local authorities are creating cycle routes, particularly on disused railways, such as the Whitehaven to Ennerdale Cycle Path, or the splendid routes in County Durham which are well worth riding. The gradients are relatively easy but some sections are stuck up on very exposed hillsides.

The Forestry Commission has mountain bike routes in most of its conservancies. Many follow routes that are bridleways, most do not.

The Border Forest Park authorities have even gone as far as building a link section dedicated to bikes and horses joining Kielder Forest on the English side with Newcastleton Forest in Scotland, and in the Great Glen between Fort William and Inverness tremendous work has been done to create the Great Glen Cycle Route, which apart from being enjoyable provides a much safer alternative to the busy A82. We can't ask more than that.

Landowners can give permission to ride on footpaths. I have used a short stretch of little used path on an organised event, but it is always best to get it in writing. They can also give permission to ride where there is no right of way at all, just as any property owner could. However you should not return to race courses unless you are certain they are a right of way. Many folk think that these one-off venues can be used at any time. They can not. Several good race venues have been lost due to competitors and friends returning to ride over private land.

Obviously you need to behave properly, and most permissions will only be given for one-off occasions, but if you are prepared to give something in return you'll often be given access. Doing the work necessary to make a track usable yourselves is a good idea. Often funds for materials, or the materials themselves are available, but manpower is the most expensive element. Working with locals and countryside rangers on repair and maintenance is another avenue to good relations. Go and support their Open Days, organisers of shows and fetes are always looking for new attractions. How about a mountain bike race around the village green, with the bunnyhop competition in the vicarage garden?

Of course all of this would appear to be a complete waste of time in Wales where many farmers, landowners and rangers have taken a wholesome dislike to anything with wheels. But this is not entirely the case. Local volunteers in Powys have cleared and improved 35 miles of unusable bridleways in the last few years, aided and abetted by the good old Forestry Commission, and there are other good works afoot in virtual secrecy at other locations in the Principality, waiting for the regime to change. Good luck.

How others would like us to behave

Horses
Anne Lee of the British Horse Society is well aware of the Mountain Bike Code of Conduct. She emphasises that horse riders are used to sharing paths, we are not in conflict and should not be so.

Mountain Bike Code of Conduct: give way to horses, they may not be under proper control. One of these, on the road up to Threlkeld Common, Cumbria, was particularly flighty

However, it would help greatly if cyclists understood horses. The beasts are totally unpredictable when alarmed so please try to give them some sort of warning. A bell or call when you are **well** away if you are coming up behind is a good idea, but bends will always be a problem. We jokingly agreed that singing might be a good idea, but the most obvious thing to do is to slow down. The best advice to bikers is self preservation. Horses are big and heavy, and not every rider is fully competent. So give them plenty of notice of your presence and plenty of room as you pass.

Gates and stiles
Wherever possible use the stile, it saves interfering with the gate. Some stiles, particularly over deer fences, are huge, so pause and consider how you are going to turn at the top so your bike doesn't foul anything on the descent. If you are in touring mode consider removing your panniers and making a couple of trips. Leave gates as you find them. If a gate is closed but unfastened just leave it like that, it might close by gravity and the farmer might open it by simply nudging it with his vehicle. If it has been tied he could wreck the gate, and public relations could suffer a similar fate.

Walkers
Alan Mattingly of the Ramblers Association made the point that there are more important issues than mountain bikers on their agenda at the moment, but has received an increasing number of complaints from members and other walkers about mountain bikers using footpaths and the association was urging local authorities to enforce the law rather more.

Elderly walkers complained about the speed and silence of bikes, so it comes back to the bell again, but he did agree that a certain element would glare or chastise you for daring to ring your bell at them, even if they were walking five abreast and blocking the road.

A final word of advice comes from Brian Thompson, Assistant Rights of Way Officer for Northumberland who strongly makes the point that as a body we should be organised, with one central voice. To him the British Mountain Bike Federation seems the obvious focus where local authorities can make contact, a unit through which mountain bikers' grievances can be channelled, otherwise we will never be consulted or included in rights of way legislation. We must have strong representation, this means adequate funding for a complete team of full time administrators.

Historic roads and trade routes

All over the world people have been travelling from place to place since the beginning of time. In many places the passage of feet, hooves and wheels have established paths, tracks and roads. Many of these developed into major highways because they followed the line of least resistance, but many have fallen into disuse and been virtually forgotten.

Even in our tiny island you can trace the history of the roads. In many areas there is evidence of established routes of the Ancient Britons, ancient trackways like the Icknield Way and its continuation the Ridgeway, which is generally accepted to be one of the oldest 'roads' in the world. The Ridgeway can be ridden for most of its length, and there is a certain satisfaction and feeling of history to be gained in following one of these old thoroughfares, although to say that you would be following exactly in the steps of the Ancient Britons might be a little presumptive. Most of these very old roads were merely well-worn trails, and in places where the ground was soft several lines developed as people sought the easiest going, a situation paralleled today on stretches of the Pennine Way and other well-travelled high paths.

Then came those great road builders, the Romans, who established a nationwide network with names such as Watling Street, Ermine Street, Akeman Street and Dere Street which even penetrated into Scotland. Unfortunately, from our point of view, they built the roads too well, their foundations and line were so good they have been constantly updated through the centuries and many comprise the trunk road system of today. But there are still one or two stretches,

like the extreme northern end of Dere Street where it crosses the Cheviot Hills, that are unmade and highly entertaining. It is worth doing a little research with a map of the Roman roads of Britain and the current OS map to see what you can discover.

After that came the development of a road system north of the Forth in Scotland in which General Wade figured largely. Again, we still use many of these roads today but some, like the Devil's Staircase in Glen Coe, have fallen into decline.

As you can appreciate, the main reason behind the road building was military, and even today the protection of frontiers lies behind the construction of new routes in difficult country. The finest examples of this were the Alpine roads built over the high passes by Napoleon Bonaparte to assist the rapid movement of his armies through the countries of Southern Europe early in the nineteenth century. In the first decade of the century he caused roads to be built over the Col du Mont Cenis, Simplon Pass, Col du Lautaret, Col du Mont Genevre, Col de Sestriere, Col de Tende and Corniche. The Simplon road in particular was a tremendous technical project that employed 6,000 men who built literally hundreds of bridges, tunnels and galleries, allegedly 613 bridges between the south end of Lago

Maggiore and Brigue. There were nine evenly spaced refuges for shelter in bad weather and a barracks on the summit.

Alongside the military significance trade developed apace. There had always been routes used for both legitimate trade and smuggling along paths and tracks in the mountains, and still are, but these new roads attracted tremendous use. The Col du Mont Cenis road, begun in 1803 and completed in 1810, was the work of 2,000 men. In the first year of opening it was used by 2,911 carriages, 14,037 carts and wagons, and 37,255 horses and mules.

Some of the more remote valleys have maintained the muletracks or sentieri until recent times and they provide excellent riding. My personal favourite is the Eisjochl or Passo Gelato, 2895m, in the Sud Tyrol. This is an internal Italian pass within sight of the Austrian border, within 10km of the spot where the Bronze Age man was found in 1990, and where you can actually ride higher than the glaciers in a fantastic situation. There is a little carrying or pushing, but unlike many of the very high Alpine routes the greatest part of your day will be spent riding.

In North America trying to follow the old stagecoach lines across the Badlands could be an interesting exercise, or even something really wild across Asia like the ancient Silk Road pioneered by Marco Polo. The route of the latter stills exists but there would appear to be little pleasure coupled to your achievement in traversing it. In the words of Julie Kett who made a crossing in 1992 'Don't do it!' They were harassed in central China and regularly spat upon, forced to barricade themselves and their bikes in their rooms in Taxhorgan, and around Islamabad even the adults threw rocks down on them. Her advice seems well founded!

Recommended areas

In addition to choosing a route for its terrain it is worth considering the timing of your trip. Despite the fact that it might be perfectly legal to ride a certain route, when conditions are too bad it could be a good decision not to visit that area in the interests of erosion and public relations. In most counties there are hard surface alternatives that won't be affected in wet periods. Use them at these times of year and keep the more delicate routes for the Summer.

It is always dangerous to recommend a particular area because others may not enjoy the same type of riding. They may prefer tours where it is never necessary to carry or push the bike, or on the other hand thoroughly enjoy the pure challenge of dragging the bike over the most demanding terrain. What follows here is a selection based on experience and enjoyment, to a greater or lesser degree!

England

North York Moors Routes to suit all abilities. Long bridleways, some superimposed on defunct railways, old lanes on the fringes of the Moors, and all types of accommodation. This is a tourist orientated area and well worth a visit. Try the big arc from Snilesworth across the head of Bilsdale, or the Westside Road over Rudland Rigg to Battersby.

Lake District Picturesque and popular. Too popular for weekend biking in the honeypot areas, but midweek and off season there is a wealth of excellent routes. Many of the higher tracks involve a lot of carrying, but if you spread your interest to the peripheral areas you will find some excellent totally ridable old lanes and roads. Try a circuit of Skiddaw using the eastern bridleways, or the old roads around Ullswater.

Wales

Elan Valley Lots of old roads and bridleways. Very stony in places. Helmet, good trackmitts and suspension recommended. Try a circuit of the Claerwen Reservoir.

Dovey Forest An infinite number of reasonably smooth roads and some terrific views which must be paid for with climbs to match. Intricate old byways well worth following weave their way between Corris and Aberangell. Test your navigational prowess.

Scotland

The Great Glen Glen Mor or Glen Albyn, all the same place, the valley between Fort William and Inverness. There is the Great Glen Cycle Route which will eventually run all the way, coast to coast, numerous mountain bike routes scattered right up the Glen, and opportunities to go really remote by striking out to the west, or southeast across Rannoch Moor. Always take your showerproofs, and a good midge repellent if you are camping.

Central Highlands For lovers of old through routes this is the place. The area east of Rannoch Moor between Pitlochry and Aviemore has a wealth of old drovers routes, whiskey trails and stalkers paths. Many are still in use and have excellent ridable surfaces, some are a bit more of a test. Try Blair Atholl to Deeside via Glen Tilt, or the Minigaig Pass just slightly further west, or go for the

big one and make them into a circuit. They are brilliant.

Europe

Austria

Austria abounds in access roads to ski stations and mountain top restaurants. Most are well surfaced like British forest roads, and for the downhill specialists the ski lifts will take your bike to the top. All the ski resorts are good areas, Hohe Tauern and the Kitzbuheler Alps especially.

Kitzbuhel Renowned for its world championship skiing downhill, it could easily stage the mountain bike version too. Both sides of the valley have lots of service roads and single track. Go valley hopping and get the train back.

Salzburgerland Easier riding, Sound of Music country, but still hilly enough to induce a good night's sleep, and you can ride into it straight from the airport.

Belgium

Belgium is bicycle mad, but it's usually the skinny tyred variety. However, there is lots to go at in the south of the country.

Ardennes Here are a number of arrowed MTB routes emanating from Phillipeville, but anywhere in the Ardennes can be entertaining,

especially after a shower of rain. The slip factor of the mud is rivalled only by the southern chalks of Salisbury Plain. Go soon before it becomes too popular.

France

France is vast, so is the choice of biking. The Alps are an obvious magnet for the hard men, but there are easier and warmer areas too. Most resorts are crowded from mid July right through August, the snow is down to 2,000m well into June, later on north facing slopes, so early September seems the best time.

Chamonix Cosmopolitan, lively, and the prospect of the Tour de Mont Blanc, a really serious challenge. As the name suggests it is a circuit of Mont Blanc, taking six to eight days entering Italy and Switzerland as well as France. The route is waymarked but becomes very busy at the height of the season. However, there are many kilometres of non TMB riding and English MTB guides in the town if you need them. (See Bibliography for Organisations).

Grand Randonnees There are several long distance walking routes through France, Grand Randonnees (GRs), many linking other European countries, and containing long sections eminently suited to mountain biking, though all contain difficult stretches in their highest parts which could be a stiff test with the bike. These make excellent 'grand' projects which could be nibbled at over several visits. The best source of information is the Federation Francaise de la Randonnee Pedestre, (see Bibliography) or the specific walking guides.

Germany

Germany has a different approach to bikes. There are waymarked and often separate cycle routes everywhere, even in the biggest cities. If you fancy long but easy rides you can follow the rivers, which isn't quite as easy as it sounds, the little cycle paths atop the flood dykes in the upper reaches of the Rhine can be real entertainment.

Bavaria The Bavarian Alps are a long range of mountains in the south. There are many unsurfaced roads and some very testing routes. It pays not to be too ambitious to begin with, choose an area and concentrate your efforts locally. Valepp is a good base.

Harz Mountains Providing what used to be the border between east and west, the Harz are richly endowed with 'Wanderwege' which can vary from forest roads to bumpy rooted paths. Great entertainment. Goslar is a good starting point.

Italy

Amazingly there were no mountain bikes in Italy a few years ago, but now the Italians have embraced off-road cycling to such a degree that 'mountain bike' is the correct Italian, not biciclette montagna.

The Italian Alps and Dolomites The best mountain biking in the world. Accessible, steep, no mud, south facing, brilliant ice cream, even marked routes. What more could you want? From Aosta in the west to Cortina d'Ampezzo in the east there is an incredible range of mountains with internal passes, some of the hairiest four-wheel-drive roads imaginable and a nation of cyclists who will cheer your every effort as you toil up the big ones. Just buy a map and go.

Garfagnana Tuscany is one of the great surprises of Italian mountain biking. The local hills, Alpi Apuane and Appennino Toscoemilliano rise to 1,800m. They have published a map locally with an official 180Km circular mountain bike tour thereon, and have virtually unlimited sunshine. May to September is the official season, but you'll want to ride early or late in the day in July because of the heat.

Norway

Norway is so different you should go at least once. Choose a limited area to explore and plan lower than usual mileages. Apart from the central mountains, the Jotunheimen, everything seems to start at sea level and rise vertically. Of course it doesn't, but it certainly seems that way. This is the hardest cycling country in Europe.

Jotunheimen A relatively small, area with many gravel roads. Surfaces not unlike Scotland with rocky eroded tracks and bouldery paths. Also like Scotland the midges can get out of hand, by the time the high tracks are snow free the gnats have licence to kill. Get off the hill before sundown.

Finnmark Most of the roads are gravel, and you'll need to use the Hurtigruta, coastal ferries, from time to time. The rewards are the midnight sun and the world's most northerly town, Hammerfest.

Spain

From the challenging northern border of the Pyrenees to the Sierra Nevada in the south Spain is vast. If you plan a nationwide crossing do it west to east with the prevailing wind at your back, otherwise it could ruin your ride.

Pyrenees There are dozens of trails in the Pyrenees. Many are old trade and smuggling routes adopted by walkers. There is a reasonable chain of mountain huts, and so much

Italy's Dolomites provide some of the best high-altitude mountain biking in the world. It's a nation of cyclists who will even pull a wheelie for the camera like this one near Rifugio Tondi, 2327m

Riding high has a fascination all of its own. Often in the mountainous areas of the world there are excellent tracks at considerable altitude, as this route through the Spanish Pyrenees shows

Ordnance Survey Map Markings

	England & Wales Landranger 1:50,000	Pathfinder 1:25,000	Outdoor Leisure 1:25,000
Road, drive or track. May or may not be a right of way	═══════════	═══════════	═══════════
Path, not a right of way, but could also be an old Byway	- - - - - - - - - - -	- - - - - - - - -	- - - - - - - -
Footpath. Right of Way, but not for bicycles. Permitted path	·················	·················	·················
Bridleway. Right of Way for bicycles. Permitted bridleway	– – – – – – – – –	– – – – – – – – –	– – – – – – – – –
Road Used as a Public Path. 99% certain to be a legal Right of Way for bicycles as most have vehicular rights	–·–·–·–·–·–	⊥ ⊤ ⊥ ⊤	⊥ ⊤ ⊥ ⊤
Byway Open to All Traffic, in other words old unclassified county roads. OK for bicycles	+ –+– + – +	+ + + +	+ + + +

Travelling fairly light in big mountain country. Day routes at lesser altitudes can be undertaken in complete safety when the weather is good. You will also get a great feeling of freedom

'undiscovered' terrain it is a must for the adventurous. The eastern end of the chain tends to be much drier than the west, but if the weather turns foul you can always escape to the fleshpots of the coastal strip.

Andalucia This area of southern Spain is highly accessible due to the number of Torremelinos bound charter flights, and can provide a challenge of whatever severity you decree. Inland from the coast accommodation can be limited in the smaller villages, but you can get details of the government owned rifugios in the mountains from the Spanish National Tourist Office. Spring is the best time to go unless you intend to tackle Europe's highest road, Pic Veleta 3392m, then you'll need to wait until well into July when the snow melts.

Switzerland

Everything in Switzerland is regulated very carefully and the restrictions on mountain biking have received more exposure than the vast number of approved routes.

The *Guide Suisse De Mountain Bike* (French/German text) has 720 pages. Quite incredible.

Eastern Switzerland The Grisons and the Engadine, particularly the southern fringes towards the Italian border provide some incredible challenges, even the tarmac passes will require the granny gears.

Highest passes Even on the permanent snow passes there are well-trodden paths. Attempting a crossing depends on how much carrying you are prepared to do and your mountaineering expertise. The Theodul Pass 3301m, has been biked several times, but the Allalin Pass 3564m, has yet to be conquered as far as I know.

North America

The variation in local restrictions pertaining to bikes has already been mentioned. Check locally before you ride. Everything is on a grand scale

Arizona The Superstitions mountain range, home of the Apaches, just east of Phoenix is worth exploring. Old trails, dry riverbeds, and ghost towns.

California You have got to ride Marin County, where it all started

Colorado Durango, dozens of ride possibilities, even 10 or so that could be called gently rolling. Abandoned jeep roads and technical single track abound. There's the World Championship Downhill course at Purgatory, and also the lure of Crested Butte.

Vermont Best in the Fall, beautiful colours, great woodland trails, but the purists claim it has a month-long mud season in the Spring - sounds just like the UK!

Guidebooks

If you are new to the sport or new to an area a guidebook can be invaluable. You know for certain (hopefully!) that someone has ridden over the route before. It might well be beyond **your** capability, but the guide should give you a good idea of the severity.

For the long distance routes you may need to rely upon walking guides, but you can get some fantastic ideas from them, not necessarily to follow the identical route but something close and modified to be more suitable for mountain bikes. My Coast to Coast route was inspired by the venerable Wainwright's pedestrian version.

Chapter 7
Navigation

Everyone can navigate, find their way about, we do it every day. How do we do it? Simply by recognising different places, features, and taking some action, such as turning left at the Post Office. We do it close to where we live practically without thinking, but the whole thing becomes more exciting when you venture into new territory.

Navigation is an essential skill for the complete mountain biker, it can be fun, fascinating and give you a tremendous sense of satisfaction. I still get a kick out of finding my way over terrain I've never covered before, knowing exactly where I am on the map and having the confidence to predict what is out of sight around the corner, and then finding I am spot on and correct. I suppose it's really an ego trip, but good navigation can save you a lot of grief when the going gets tough.

The ancient peoples of the world relied solely on observation for navigation, they were finding their way about the globe for centuries

before any navigational instruments were invented, being guided only by the sun, the moon, the stars and their surroundings.

Today we rely heavily on maps, which are not always correct, because apart from errors they simply become out of date. Trees grow to maturity and are felled for timber, as a result a wood that is marked on the map doesn't exist any more. A new road is built, or a housing estate is established where once it was all green fields. There is constant change, to cope with it you must be able to navigate.

It is possible to complete a journey without ever knowing where you are in relation to the starting point. It is so easy to become totally absorbed in your immediate surroundings, but you need to look all around you, and relate your present position to the whole area, just in case you need to make an instant decision enforced by mechanical failure or injury.

Don't leave the navigating to

someone else, although it is a change to have a day off occasionally. Even if you are not the one with the map take an interest and keep a check on the situation as you may be called upon to take over at any time.

Observation

Perhaps I shouldn't admit it, but the first time I went to Norway I navigated my way through the mountains of the Jotunheimen without a compass, with a map whose scale was 1:200,000 or even smaller. I didn't carry a compass because I didn't know how to use one, but had excellent observation and was pretty good at relating the map to the ground, or so I thought, until a welcome flat bit turned out to be a frozen lake! We never got lost but had a couple of epic struggles across snowy cols, and took the precaution of joining a guided party to cross one of the highest glaciers. I didn't know any better at the time, I had always navigated this way, by observation alone. It's a skill I've never lost, and still use it more than anything else.

Even when conditions become dire and the compass is necessary, observation still has its part to play, in fact it is of paramount importance, whether you are going to stick to tracks and well-worn ways, or whether you choose to caress the limits and venture where no wheel has gone before. Basically if you don't see the track or landmark and relate to it you'll get lost.

What do you observe? Anything, and everything: salient features like hills, roads, tracks, streams and rivers, which can either help your journey or bar the way. But as you extend your horizons you'll step into the province of changes in vegetation and ancient gateposts standing alone.

Being on wheels we tend to follow the larger tracks, simply because they are more ridable and there is a limit to how much enjoyment we can derive from carrying a bike all day, but every now and then what was marked on the map as a bridleway disappears and your observation is put to the test. Naturally you would refer to the map, but in remote hill terrain the lesser rights of way are often only good approximations simply because the track barely exists any more, and we must look for ancient signs. Frequently you will encounter gates,

Occasionally, as at the col beneath Creagan Dubh, An Slugan, Isle of Skye, only a gate remains to confirm the route. No fence, the gate is your only clue to the route ahead

often overgrown and long neglected, on the line of a track where it pierces a fence line, older tracks have only the gateposts left – they may be rotting and lichen covered – but they are still reliable sentinels to confirm the route.

Thoroughfares are soon reclaimed by the vegetation when neglected, and are sometimes invaded by sphagnum moss or rushes which can indicate the line as well as any signpost. On other occasions the only hint may be a slightly different colouration of the grass, difficult to discern in summer, but usually easier in winter. Remote moorland routes are often highlighted by a covering of snow in the winter months.

Travel always has some impact on the terrain, whether by foot or wheeled vehicle. The old roads invariably run through depressions worn by the various passengers, many are outstanding but some need the low morning, evening, or winter sun to bring them to your attention. Look well ahead, even to the other side of the valley and fix the route in your mind.

Develop the overall picture of the route in your mind, don't become

An overgrown and neglected gate on the line of a track where it pierces a fence line on Thirlwall Common, Northumberland

bogged down by the problems immediately ahead, they need to be surmounted, but never lose sight of the grand plan, the entire tour. Often in high Alpine situations avalanches demolish the tracks, or at least cover them with so much debris that diversions become necessary. As you climb take note of the other side of the valley, is there a path on the far side you could use as an alternative? Is there another track on your side that may not have been affected? Or would it be wiser to turn back before you get wiped out as well as the track?

Using maps

It is worth quoting the words of that great adventurer and author Robert Louis Stevenson with regard to maps:

'I am told there are people who do not care for maps and find it hard to believe ... here is an inexhaustible fund of information for any man with eyes to see or twopence worth of imagination to understand with.'

Every map is made up of hundreds of bits of information. Not all of it is relevant to mountain biking, but most of it is. Practise recognising the symbols. On occasions I have gone as far as cutting the key off a map and pasting it onto a small piece of card so I didn't need to open the map out fully when I wanted to check something – a great help on a windy day.

The scale of map you use will depend on two factors, the length of journey you are about to undertake, and what is available! In the UK you can buy Ordnance Survey (OS) maps virtually anywhere, but in many countries the quality of maps available is abysmal, and the scales don't just stick to 1:25,000 or 1:50,000, you get 1:30,000, 1:40,000 and tourist maps which are little better than sketch maps which don't appear to have a scale at all!

OS Landranger maps (1:50,000 scale) have the advantage of covering quite a large area, but seem to be especially designed to have all the best mountain bike routes overlapping onto at least one other map! All the bridleways are marked but it is often difficult to judge whether the route is simply a right of way or whether there is an actual track on the ground too.

Pathfinder maps (1:25,000 scale) usually give you a better idea of the existence of tracks on the ground, cover a much smaller area, but are particularly useful in foul weather because they have the fences and walls marked.

Many of the Outdoor Leisure 1:25,000 series give you the best of both worlds by being printed on both sides, so you lose nothing in the area covered, and they usually feature the countryside of most interest to us in any case. There are currently 32 in the series covering most of the popular leisure and recreation areas in the country from Torridon in the far north, to the Isles of Scilly in the far southwest.

Every cartographer has his own favourite symbols, and different countries have different demands. When using a foreign map for the first time try to ride a route that includes as many of the track types as possible, an assimilation route. That way you will get a clearer picture of what is marked and what is ridable.

As a general rule in Alpine

countries tracks marked with a continuous red line are ridable unless the gradient is too steep, those marked with a dashed red line are only ridable downhill, and the paths marked by red dots are a definite carry. The crosses signify the famous *via ferrata*, very steep paths or rock climbs protected by metal ladders or steel ropes. Learn what all the symbols mean as soon as possible.

Obtaining 1:25,000 or similar scale maps of foreign countries in the UK is often very difficult although all the Alpine countries produce them. They are always available locally when you get there, often at the little street corner tobacco kiosks, but this doesn't help with planning. We tend to gravitate towards the more mountainous areas, so good climbing shops are often the best UK source of maps, and of course the relevant national tourist office should be able to point you in the direction of stockists.

Before I went to Italy for the first time I planned most of my activities with the aid of a 1:200,000 Touring Club Italiano map which showed many of the high off-road passes. They often aren't actually off-road in the purest sense, in the high mountains everyone travels by means of good four-wheel drive vehicles. It's either that or walk, or mountain bike, but when you get there buy your local 1:25,000 (or

thereabouts) map and you'll see many more off-road challenges which will destroy your well-laid plans.

Protecting the map
It is always a good idea to protect your map from dampness, either rain or sweat. Purpose made map cases are quite good but most of them tend to work their way around your body and dangle in among the controls, the last thing you want on the best descent of the day. Avoid cheap map cases, they usually leak. Some bar bags, such as Karrimor and Vaude have a detachable map case which sits on the top. Whether it's a good idea to read as you ride is debatable, but at least the map is readily available.

The cheapest, and most effective, system of map protection is a stout plastic bag, it will also hold your 2B pencil and sharpener without suffering serious damage, and even if it does it is easily replaced. The Italian Tabacco maps always come in a plastic envelope but it is not quite good enough to keep out the rain; German Kompass maps, which you'll find in all the German speaking areas of the Alps come in a durable wallet that overlaps the size of the map to the point where you will be most unfortunate if water gets in, but I still put mine in the plastic bag.

I did a rough map protection

survey at the Polaris International MTB Challenge. Most competitors favoured the plastic bag, very few used professionally produced map cases, and most that did had modified them in some way, a couple of top 10 finishers had gone for lamination, and the rest of the protectors were trying spray-on waterproofing agents with varying degrees of success.

Lamination comes in varying weights. The simplest method is to cover it with Contac, an adhesive transparent film you can buy at hardware stores. It makes the map quite bulky, particularly if you do the job properly and laminate both sides, but is totally effective.

A much lighter film applied by Prontoprint works very well, and I have seen a beautifully clear system used by a couple of lads from an advertising agency who had cut their maps into sections to apply it. Unfortunately it was unfoldable so they carried a roll of maps nearly the size of a sleeping mat, and as you might have expected, one of the references needed was right on the edge which necessitated using two of their monster sheets for a while. No doubt their maps will last forever, but they were a trifle difficult to use! Make sure your system is flexible.

Any system of lamination requires either felt tipped marker pens or chinagraph pencils to mark

Understanding map scales

Scale	Actual measurements	Comment
1:10,000	1cm = 100m	Too large a scale for mountain biking. Too small an area covered
1:25,000	1cm = 250m	Essential in very mountainous areas Large enough for accurate representation of track/path quality
1:30,000	1cm = 300m	Excellent. Usually produced for popular Alpine tourist areas
1:40,000	1cm = 400m	Good scale for hilly country
1:50,000	1cm = 500m	Good area covered, usually ample detail for mountain biking
1:100,000	1cm = 1,000m (1Km)	Still good enough for touring, but use only off-road in mountains if nothing else available
1:200,000	1cm = 2,000m (2Km)	Planning maps

the maps, but if you always use a laminate this should be no problem.

Estimating distances

The types of routes we undertake are unlikely to be signposted, although it is surprising what you find in the Alps and the Scottish Highlands, but in general the distances are omitted, so the estimation is down to you, and you'll probably want to do this before you leave home or base in any case.

Draw your route on the map, a 2B pencil is best because it is nice and black and easy to erase.

Sometimes this really helps at the end of a long tiring day when you're not thinking as sharply as you should, and if you mark the junctions nice and sharply, or even exaggerate them a little, you'll not miss them. Also by doing this you will look elsewhere on the map to a greater or lesser degree, and subconsciously be aware of alternatives should the need to escape arise.

The most accurate way to estimate the distance is to run an opisometer, or map measuring wheel, along the route, but in doing this there are three points to consider. First check the accuracy of the opisometer against the scale on the map, neither of mine are

accurate. I must multiply the reading on one by 0.8 to get a correct reading, and the other by 0.883. Second, if you have a type bearing several different scales make sure you read the right one, and the third point is to bear in mind that you are measuring a flat plan view of the countryside, the contours will add to the overall distance.

Slopes and gradients

Because road gradients are usually expressed as a percentage it is important to understand just what this means. The percentages are not the same as the inclination of the slope in degrees. (See Fig B)

The distance added by the angle of the terrain in most cases is not great, but once it exceeds a slope angle of 20° it will become significant. The following table explains.

Slope angle	Additional distance travelled
10 °	1.5%
20 °	6%
30 °	15%

Slopes greater than 30° are usually unridable, and very rare on most tracks, but if you do venture into this severe class of terrain, distance covered is not the major consideration, what will really

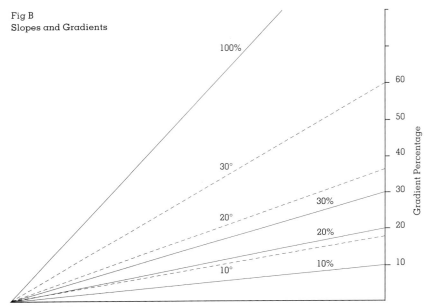

Fig B
Slopes and Gradients

100%

30°

20°

10°

30%

20%

10%

60

50

40

30

20

10

Gradient Percentage

INCLINATION - Degrees

the ground as you clock up the kilometres, and some of the top speeds are incredible!

Compare your estimates with the reality when you return, try to assess where the discrepancies arose, did you stick to the planned route? Were there any diversions? Were the tracks used actually the same as on the map? Or did you retrace for any reason? If so revise your next estimates accordingly.

Make sure you don't inadvertently switch off your computer when lifting the bike over stiles or obstructions, or when carrying on the steepest climbs.

Route cards

You can prepare a route card before your journey which will act as a reminder, and perhaps as reassurance late in the day, giving distances to salient points and even possible escape routes on the back. That way if disaster, mechanical or physical, strikes you've got the basis of a plan which can either be adopted or modified to suit the incident.

The example shown here features a route in the north Pennines circumnavigating the highest points, Great Dun Fell 847m, Cross Fell 893m, and the source of the River Tees as well as visiting the source of the River South Tyne.

concern you will be the overall difficulty of the route and the time expected to take to complete it. One solution might be to get the ski lift to the top, then try to ride down!

Kilometre squares

The national grid system superimposed upon British Ordnance Survey maps is divided into kilometre squares. This even applied when the standard scale was one inch to the mile, a great piece of forward thinking. Not all maps have a grid system of this type superimposed, but you will find that all of the Alpine cartographers have

used it. Occasionally the grids are 2km squares, but your familiarity with the system will stand you in good stead all over Europe.

Estimation is easy using the grid without any sort of instrument if the track is straight, simply count the kilometre squares. If the route lies directly across a square it is obviously one kilometre, the diagonal is 1.5km, and you can estimate the other wiggles from that.

I have calibrated my cycle computer in kilometres and always prepare my route cards metrically too, to give a uniform system. Apart from the accuracy achieved using the smaller units of measurement, you feel that you are really covering

INTER is the distance in kilometres between adjacent features,

DONE is the distance already covered, and

TO DO as the name suggests, is how far it is to the end.

TR Turn Right

SO Straight On

In this case the only Escape Routes are to retrace or curtail the route by following the ridge from Great Dun Fell to Cross Fell, which believe it or not, we did on one occasion in the depth of winter when a torn muscle (mine!) dictated that any alternative to wading through waist high snow with the bike was desirable! The decision will be dictated by the circumstances.

Relating the map to the ground

If you are following roads or well-defined tracks there are few problems. There may even be signposts, but it is essential you always know precisely where you are. Hold the map in front of you and turn it around until you line up your drawn route with the real road in front of you. Once you set off along it you can mark off junctions and other features as you pass them. Setting the map like this is easy if you are travelling north because all

Sample route card

	Inter	Done	To do
Garrigill (Ford) 86/745413	0	0	45.2
Dorthgill (Good tarmac ends)	3.7	3.7	41.5
Tynehead 558m	3.3	7.0	38.2
Moor House bridge 537m (onto singletrack)	2.3	9.3	35.9
Great Dun Fell col 755m (onto tarmac)	4.8	14.1	31.1
Knock, Close Houses 215m TR	6.4	20.5	24.7
Blencarn 175m 91/636312 TR	6.8	27.3	17.9
Kirkland SO onto white	1.9	29.2	16.0
Cross Fell Coffin Road col 781m	5.8	35.0	10.2
Garrigill	10.2	45.2	0

(28.1 miles)

NB Use stiff card which is more durable than paper, especially when stuffed into a sweaty pocket, laminate it with adhesive film or slot it into a neat plastic bag to protect it. The laminating system has the advantage that the route card is all one entity and easier to read.

the place names lie on the map neatly in front of you. However, if you are travelling south all the writing is upside down. This takes a little getting used to, but if the map is correctly set in relation to its surroundings it will always lie along the same axis. It is you who are actually standing at the other side. (See Fig C)

With this system you do not really need a compass, but it only works when you can see your surroundings. As mentioned earlier, one of the best ways of keeping tabs on your position is to tick off features on the map as you pass them: junctions are obvious,

buildings are good markers and streams focus your attention on the geographical features which become more important as the going becomes more remote. No terrain is featureless, but some areas such as the Border Ridge in the Cheviot Hills, have sections that are so similar to one another, and rounded summits that at times seem to defy identification to the newcomer, that it becomes essential to mark the map regularly. Even bridleway junctions are no more than rabbit tracks, and you become forced to measure the distances with the scale on your compass, then tie them into the reading on your cycle computer.

Travelling North

Travelling South

Fig C
Note that the map is set in relation to the ground and will always lie along the same axis regardless of the direction travelled

This is accuracy we bikers can achieve far better than the walkers. It is also an idea to write your time of passing on the map, then after a couple of hours you'll be able to estimate how long the route is going to take, and make any decision about when to finish to get you off the hill before darkness. This can be especially useful on short winter days.

Make a point of identifying and naming all the hills around you, this is an excellent way of focussing your attention, but could turn you into an horrendous bore in years to come!

Contours

Contours are imaginary lines joining points of equal height above sea level. On OS Landranger maps they are marked at 10m intervals, and on the Pathfinders at 5m vertical intervals. With these intervals it is possible that the smaller ups and downs can be lost, but because we mainly use tracks and roads this should be no great problem, and even if our route diminishes to a sheep track such undulations will be the least of our concerns. This more detailed map interpretation really comes into its own when you become involved in serious off-road routes.

It can be seen on Fig D that the lines are closer together on the steeper side of the hill. This is obviously more difficult riding.

Learn the different characteristic contour patterns for different physical features. Valleys are usually easy to identify as they often have a stream or river in the bed, and often provide the only shelter from the wind on bleak mountain routes. Use a known hill as your standard, remember the density of the contours, then relate this to your proposed route.

Fig D
In the plan view note how the contour lines are closer together on the steep side. Heights may be omitted where they confuse important detail, or there is simply not space

Contouring

Ideal contouring is being able to maintain the same height while still making progress towards your destination. The best example of this are the roads around reservoirs, but they may still seem to have two or three horrific little climbs in them. Don't you just hate it when they do that? There are more fine examples on the monster Alpine road passes, and occasionally the off-road versions too, where they gently but remorselessly climb right to the head of the valley then contour all the way back along the far side. The track goes on for mile after mile, but at least you are riding. If it went straight up the mountainside to the top you would need climbing boots, if not ropes too. If there is a less steep option, it stands a better chance of being ridable.

Contour interruptions

When you get into really serious mountain journeys you'll have the occasional carry around outcrops, cliffs, or even across extensive screes. Honing your symbol recognition and your planning skills will enable you to devise routes where the carrying is made easier by passing these obstacles on the right so the bike (if you usually carry it on your right shoulder, which most folk do) is out in space as opposed to colliding with the rock or hillside.

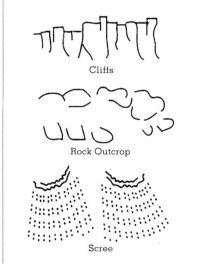

Cliffs

Rock Outcrop

Scree

Fig E
Remember the differences and how they'll affect your ability to stay on the bike

Fig E shows the OS symbols for rocky outcrops, cliffs and scree. Note that the outcrops have continuous lines, particularly around the base, and the cliffs have a solid line along the top. You can often weave through a series of outcrops, but there is no way you can ride down a cliff! Many mountain paths traverse screes, and often the surface is quite good, but if you are laden at all it is advisable to dismount and walk across. The consequences of a fall could be quite severe.

Map references

A map reference is a point which can be identified on a map by using the horizontal and vertical co-ordinates of the grid, no matter how vague they may be. British and Swiss Ordnance survey maps have a very precise grid system and are readily available, so you can be very precise in your directions, but smaller scale maps which cover a larger area often only have the lines of longitude and latitude overprinted with a numerical or alphabetical key in the border margins. Using these co-ordinates isn't as accurate for the average biker, but will still suffice for most purposes.

You only need map references for passing on information to others, but they can be very important. If you can give the police or mountain rescue services an accurate reference of an incident it will help enormously. They can be used to give the precise starting point of a route, or even used to define the whole route as some guidebooks do, they are the means of defining checkpoints in orienteering competitions such as the Polaris International MTB Challenge, and of course they are used in navigational exercises.

It is possible that there will be more than one publisher of maps for a particular area, so it is important to include details of the map you are referring to with the initial reference when you give instructions for a route. For example, Spiterstulen hostel in the Norwegian Jotunheimen could be found from, Kummerly & Frey 1:325,000 Central Norway 1,18BQ, or Deutsche Heereskarte 1:50,000 E30W Gjende, 401503. Two different systems for exactly the same place.

However, let us consider the British Ordnance Survey (OS) maps. The system is precise and can be readily adapted to virtually anything else, you could even draw your own grid on a sketch map, as long as the other party had a copy.

OS maps are overprinted with lines that represent the National Grid. The whole country is divided into 100km squares, which are then subdivided into 1km squares. Unlike the lines of longitude the grid lines do not converge, so you will appreciate that there will be only one grid line that actually points due north. This is the central line which coincides with the line of longitude two degrees west which runs from a point near Poole in Dorset, through Berwick upon Tweed and just east of Aberdeen. Obviously there will be a slight difference in all the others, each OS sheet having the deviation noted in the North Points section of the key. There will be further explanation in the sections dealing with Compass Work. For the purposes of map references we deal only with the grid.

The one kilometre squares are further subdivided into tenths to give a six figure map reference for a 100m square. This is sufficient for most of our needs because you can usually see for 100m all around you, but if more accuracy is needed occasionally halves or an intermediate five are added. The other part of the reference not affected has a zero added. For example, a standard map reference 754583 would become 75455830.

However, any six figure reference is duplicated in all the other 100km squares, so to be totally unique, the 100km square reference should be added, which you will find in the margin of the map, and the full reference would then be

NY754583. More usually the Landranger sheet number is used, in that case it would appear as 86/754583.

The grid numbering and consequently the map references are the same on the 1:25,000 Pathfinder and Outdoor Leisure maps.

The vertical grid lines are known as Eastings because they are numbered eastwards, and make up the first three numbers of a six figure reference, followed by three figures of the horizontal element, the Northings.

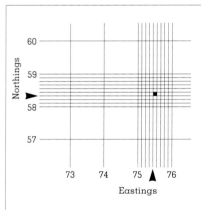

Fig F
Map ref for the 100m square 754583. The full reference is NY754583 or if using the Landranger sheet number 86/754583

Plotting an Ordnance Survey map reference

1 Read the letters identifying the 100km square from the map eg NY, or quote the sheet number, 86.

2 Quote the Eastings, which are the vertical lines numbering from left to right, or eastwards, either estimating the tenths of the 1km square or measuring them with a romer, or compass 754

3 Quote the Northings, which are the horizontal lines, numbering from the bottom up 583

4 The full reference will be either NY754583 or 86/754583

The compass

Do you need a compass? Yes. Well probably. I always used to put mine in the bumbag and forget about it, until one day I needed it in dense cloud and it wasn't there. I have overcome that problem by wearing a Suunto wrist compass, putting it on just as you would a watch, you need to be reasonably competent to use one, but I haven't lost it yet.

It is when conditions are at their worst, or you've ridden yourself into a hopeless situation, that the compass comes into its own. A good compass has many features, learn what they are and what they do, on a nice day when you have plenty of time. Leaving it until you need it is too late.

There are compasses available for almost every specialist pursuit from yachting to rally driving, diving to hang-gliding, and I suppose the baseplate type we use has an

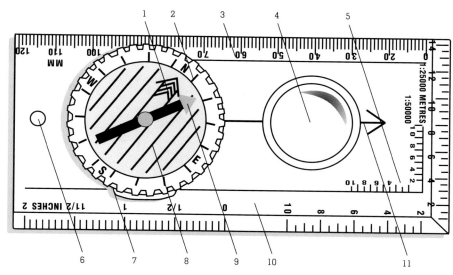

Fig G

1 Orientating arrow
2 Graduated movable bezel
3 Scale
4 Magnifying lens
5 Romer for grid reference
6 Hole for carrying cord
7 Compass housing
8 Orientating lines
9 Compass needle - North end red
10 Base plate
11 Direction of travel arrow

element of speciality too. Suunto and Silva have models to suit every level of competence, are easy to use, and justifiably still the most popular.

Every compass has several features, some are essential, some are desirable. Cost as always will have a bearing on the type you buy, so consider the following:

Essential easy to read, easy to handle
–you might need to use it while wearing gloves
robust, not too big, but large enough to use in the dark, lightweight, liquid filled, so the needle settles quickly.
Desirable romer for map references
metric scale
protractor bezel
lockable adjustment to facilitate setting magnetic variation.

Care

A compass is a precision scientific instrument. When you are not using it put it in its case. If it doesn't have one, two small pieces of sleeping mat taped together make an excellent wallet, both weatherproof and shockproof. Store it away from electrical equipment or magnets.

Use

The compass needle is a small magnet, designed to respond to the earth's magnetic field. Any other magnetic source, if close enough to the compass, will affect the reading. Even small objects like a watch, or anything containing ferrous metal can have a considerable effect, so stand away from your bike when using it.

There are natural hazards too,

certain rocks have magnetic qualities, the Scafell massif, Cumbria, creates occasional anomalies, and the Coolins of Skye are so powerful the OS map carries a warning to treat compass bearings with caution. Fortunately the 'ridable' routes through Glen Sligachan and Strath Mor are well defined (for Skye!).

Deviation

The compass needle is a magnet and will be affected by any magnetic field or ferrous object as we have already said. That's why they are made from plastics, aluminium or brass, and why you step away from your bike to take readings, to eliminate deviation, but there are greater influences.

True North

True North and South are the

geographic poles: the points where the earth's axes meet on the surface. In the northern hemisphere the direction of the North Pole is indicated by the Pole Star which can

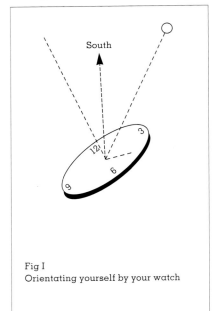

Fig H
Finding True North by the stars. The Great Bear is also known as The Plough and the Dipper

point the hour hand at the sun. Now bisect the angle between the hour hand and twelve o' clock on the dial. This will point due south. During British Summer Time, April

west. In reality there are few places on mainland Britain where the deviation is more than two degrees east or west, and even in the Outer Hebrides it is only four degrees.

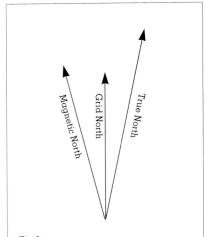

Fig J
Magnetic North about 6° west of Grid North in 1989 decreasing by about half a degree in the next three years. Depending where you are in the country, True North may be east or west of Grid North. Check your map

be found by following the Pointers in the constellation of The Plough, Great Bear or Dipper, all the same system, what you call it will depend where you live. (See Fig H)

In all fairness True North is of little use to us unless we are caught out on a cloudless starry night without a compass.

You can also orientate yourself without a compass using the sun and your watch during the day. (See Fig I) Hold your watch horizontal and

to October, bisect the angle between the hour hand and one o'clock. OK, so you've got a digital watch, simply draw an accurate clock face bearing the current time in the margin of your map and do it that way.

Grid North

Ordnance Survey maps are orientated to Grid North which differs slightly from True North except along longitude two degrees

Magnetic North

The earth has its own magnetic field within which a suspended magnetised object, such as a compass needle, will align itself. Unfortunately the Magnetic North Pole does not coincide with the Geographical North Pole (True North), and what is more, it moves! Fortunately the movement can be predicted. It is currently somewhere in the north of Canada. From Britain it is currently about sixdegrees west of Grid North, decreasing by about half a degree every three years. Naturally this Magnetic deviation needs to be allowed for because it differs from the National Grid. You will find the relevant angle in the key of any OS map.

Since Magnetic North is to the west of Grid North in this country, the compass or magnetic bearing is always the greater of the two. (See Fig J) Some top flight compasses have a lockable adjustment whereby all your readings will automatically allow for the magnetic deviation, so you don't need to add or subtract the six or so degrees at every reading. A worthwhile feature.

Setting the map with the compass

Do this with one hand if you can, that way you are forced to keep the map and the compass together.

Turn both the compass and the map so that both the grid lines and the red end of the compass needle point north. Just do it roughly at first. It doesn't matter how the baseplate is lying, look through it to align the needle with the grid lines. (See Fig K)

Once you've set the map roughly you can then refine your setting by allowing for magnetic variation, the exact deviation

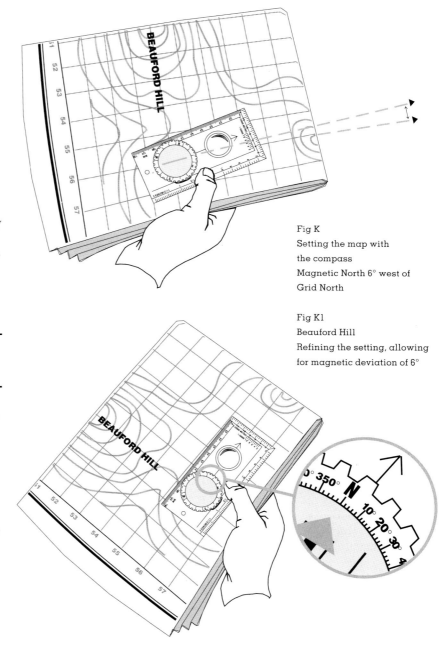

Fig K
Setting the map with the compass
Magnetic North 6° west of Grid North

Fig K1
Beauford Hill
Refining the setting, allowing for magnetic deviation of 6°

calculated from the 'North Points' section of the key for that particular map, using the graduated movable bezel of the compass.

Again it seems easier if you are facing north, but so long as the north end (top) of the map is to the north and the compass is aligned correctly you can be where you like in relation to the map, just as in Fig C, Setting the map in relation to the ground, only this time you have the compass to help, a great boon in confusing terrain or darkness.

Taking a compass bearing from the map is easier when you know for definite where you are. There's nothing better than a triangulation pillar

Taking a compass bearing from the map

The situation where this can be useful is when you know where you are, point A, you know where you want to go, point B, but there is a choice of routes, or the mist has come down and you can't see your destination or the end of this leg. You can get a similar situation occasionally when coming down off the tops, when the point in the valley you are aiming for cannot be seen and there is a choice of tracks. Late in the day you don't want to be expending more energy than you need to, and wrong route choice will invariably require that.

Use the long edge of the compass baseplate to join up where you are, point A, with your objective, point B. (See Fig L) Make sure the direction of travel arrow is pointing in the direction you want to go, A to B presumably.

Keep the base plate still and revolve the compass housing until the inner orientating lines are parallel with the grid lines on the map, and make sure the big orientating arrow is pointing north with the map. Otherwise you could be 180° out and travelling back the way you came!

The angle of bearing you need will be shown on the graduated bezel. This is the bearing related to Grid North.

Elaine Hopley resting at 310 metres beneath Maol Chean-Dearg, Wester Ross, Scotland

A cairn of this size should be shown on the map. The radio mast in the far distance is an excellent marker. If it's civil it will be on the map, alas if it has military significance, it may not

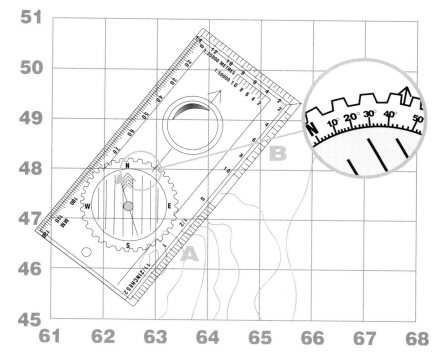

Left: Fig L
Taking a compass bearing from the map. Align the compass with your direction of travel A to B, then revolve the housing so the orientating lines are parallel with the grid lines on the map. Make sure the orientating arrow is pointing north. Ignore the actual compass needle at this time

Fig L1
Now add the 6 degrees for magnetic deviation. This is now the exact magnetic bearing you will travel along. Grid bearing of 45+ magnetic deviation of 6° = magnetic bearing of 51°

The next step is to add the magnetic deviation, again found in the North Points section of your OS map, in this case six degrees. (See Fig L1)

The magnetic deviation is always added to the grid bearing in the British Isles because, as you know, the Magnetic North Pole is somewhere near Hudson Bay in Northern Canada, which is west of the British Isles, and since bearings are always measured in a clockwise direction, the **magnetic** bearing will always be a few degrees more than the bearing you've established from the grid.

Now do a visual check if possible. You'll know where north lies from your compass, estimate the angle just to make sure you're not miles out. If you are, do it again. Of course if it is misty, cloudy or dark, you're cream crackered. In those situations you just have to trust the compass and your expertise. That's why you practised on a nice day.

All that remains now is to follow the magnetic bearing you've set on your compass. You can put the map away for the time being.

Travelling on a bearing

Hold the compass in front of you with the direction of travel arrow pointing directly ahead. Then turn around until the compass needle is lying directly over the orientating arrow, with the red end of the needle pointing to the north point on the bezel. (See Fig M)

All you have to do is keep it there and ride in the direction of travel arrow. Do not follow the compass needle, simply keep it

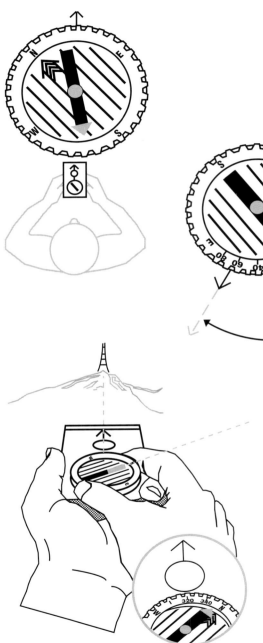

aligned over the orientating arrow.

Walkers have a distinct advantage over bikers when the weather is so foul you need to travel with your compass held out in front of you. If it is that bad, why not do the same, wheel your bike along carrying your compass well away from it in your free hand, or even stopping from time to time, stepping away from the bike (remember the effect of ferrous metals on the compass needle) and taking a reading. It is all too easy to drift off line when riding over rough terrain. Keep an eye on your distance travelled, and if necessary re-establish your bearing.

In reality it is quite dangerous to attempt to ride on a bearing. In any off-road situation you need all your concentration to choose an effective line. If you are reduced to travelling on a bearing, surely the most important thing is to navigate your way to safety, the time taken to do this is of secondary importance.

Compass to map

Sometimes it may be necessary to take a compass bearing and transfer it to the map to establish where you are, or perhaps identify a mountain out of interest. Obviously it is the reverse of what we have just done.

Point the direction of travel arrow at your chosen feature and turn the compass housing until the

51°

Fig M
Direction of Travel
Magnetic North 51°
Orientating yourself and travelling on a magnetic bearing, turn around until the compass needle is lying directly over the orientating arrow but follow the direction of the travel arrow

Fig N
Taking a compass bearing from a chosen feature

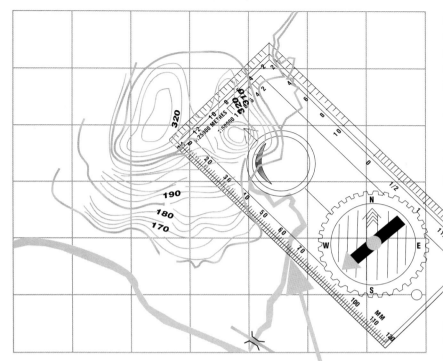

Fig N1 Transferring the compass bearing to the map. Don't forget to subtract the magnetic variation

YOU ARE HERE

orientating arrow lies aligned and directly underneath the compass needle. (See Fig N) The reading on the graduated bezel opposite travel arrow line will be your magnetic bearing.

To get your grid bearing this time you must **subtract** the magnetic deviation. Eg 324° - 6° = 318°

Set this on the graduated bezel.

Now place the compass on the map with the orientating lines parallel to the grid lines, again making sure the north point of the bezel is pointing to the north of the map.

Slide the compass across the map until one of the long sides coincides with your chosen feature, then follow the line of the edge back to see where it intersects your track. It is most important that at all times the direction of travel arrow is pointing in the direction of your chosen feature. (See Fig N1)

If you haven't a clue where you are, you can take bearings on a number of features, three minimum, and locate yourself in the triangle this produces. This is called resection. (See Fig O) Practise with a piece of graph paper and a protractor at home first.

Escape routes

The main reason for carrying a map is to find your way. Probably the most important occasion when it will be used will be to devise an escape route.

It is not always possible to plan a route with an escape alternative but it should be borne in mind, not in a negative vein, but simply as part of your expertise as an advanced mountain biker. This is particularly important in winter when there are fewer daylight hours, usually colder weather conditions and less room for manoeuvre.

Escape routes are usually demanded by:
  Injury or illness
  Mechanical breakage or malfunction
  Sudden change in the weather

No matter what the cause the usual answer is to get off the hill by the quickest and easiest route. This is why a good map of the area is essential. Plan the escape route most

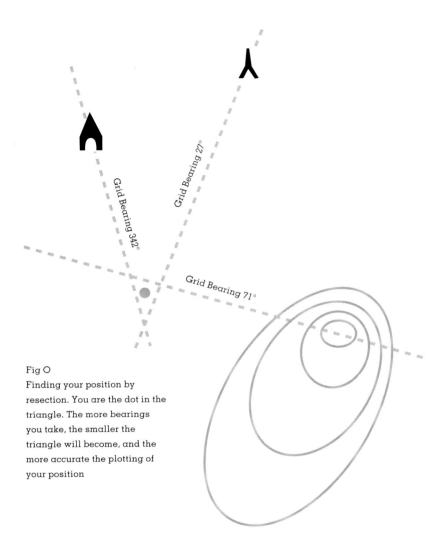

Fig O
Finding your position by
resection. You are the dot in the
triangle. The more bearings
you take, the smaller the
triangle will become, and the
more accurate the plotting of
your position

gear mechanism or an unfixable
snapped chain could simply demand
a route that can be freewheeled,
with assistance from companions on
the climbs! That's when you find
your real friends. An unexpected
change in the weather like a spring
blizzard can chase you off the tops
when you are fully fit and
mechanically perfect, so you see that
there could be a demand for three
different types of routes to suit the
circumstances.

Tiredness is one of the most
frequent causes of curtailment, then
the answer is obvious, the easiest
way home. There is a common
factor in all of these, the map, make
sure you always take one, and know
where you are all the time. This
cannot be over emphasised.

Place names

Place to place is the most obvious
system of navigation, but what do
place names convey? There are
many regional patterns, and different
names for the same features in
different parts of the country.
Consider the Welsh llyn, the
Scottish lochan, the Cumbrian tarn
and the Northumbrian lough. They
are all the same collections of water.

There must be at least one Black
Hill in every county in England.
Plan a route to take in a place with a
magic name. Take an interest in the

appropriate to whatever has
precipitated the action, forget the
original aims of the day, the most
important thing now is getting off
the hill safely.

The shortest way down is not

usually the safest, and often not the
quickest by bike. Retreat enforced
by illness or injury will certainly
demand the easiest route down,
whereas mechanical problems of a
minor nature, such as a wrecked

Gaelic place names, Welsh, Irish and Scottish, but you will probably be able to spell them correctly before you can pronounce them to the satisfaction of the locals!

Some place names capture your imagination. Dollywagon Pass, Note o' the Gate, Wheel Causeway, The Heart's Toe. They may be disappointing when you get there, but if there's an off-road challenge involved in reaching them can you refuse it?

Navigational aids

We have looked at maps and compasses which are long standing aids to navigation, but from the mountain biker's point of view one of the most recent inventions, the cycle computer, ranks with these traditional items in usefulness.

Even the simplest computer will give an accurate check on distance when calibrated correctly, which is a fantastic help on long off-road routes. It is useful to record the distances on your map from time to time, just in case the instrument is inadvertently switched off when carrying your bike over an obstruction, or it may be knocked off in a spill. If you don't already possess a computer put it on your Christmas list.

Decisions! Swinhope Moor, Northumberland, do you take a wandering snow covered track across the moor, with the inevitable stops for compass checks, or the easy option of the road? It might be more sensible in these conditions to take the easy way home

Chapter 8
River crossings

On many occasions I have been accused of being unable to plan a route that doesn't contain at least one ford, but there is a difference between using a track that has a ford (or two!) and the necessity to ford a river.

Fording rivers is an emergency procedure in which there is always an element of risk, particularly to non-swimmers.

You don't get any drag from the bike in the water if you shoulder it

Fords

Official fords can vary from manicured crossings with concrete bases, which are even and usually shallow, to the merest suggestion that a ford exists or more accurately used to exist, in the days of horses and carts with wheels of five feet diameter. There is a beauty like this near Bardon Mill on the River South Tyne, where the old entry on the north side can still be seen, and also the exit, but even in summer you would be plunged immediately into two feet of water, and a spring crossing doesn't even bear thinking about. Fortunately there is a footbridge alongside which is often a feature at the more major crossings of byways and unclassified roads.

Spates or any fast flowing situations will often roll stones onto otherwise clean ford bottoms, and just because it was OK yesterday doesn't mean it will be the same today. The bridge is always safer.

Even in summer, or especially in summer, fords can be treacherous, algae loves the merest covering of water and any shallow ford can be very slippery. Keep the bike straight as you cross and avoid any deviation if at all possible.

The Allt a Chaoil-Reidhe near Culra Bothy, Inverness-shire, Scotland, where the rocks are protruding from the water. It is often possible to use the bike as extra support as you hop from stone to stone, but watch out for the green mossy ones in summer and those with glazed icy fringes in winter

Alternatives

Just about anything is preferable to wading across a swollen river with a bike, in fact it is so dangerous it should only be undertaken in the most dire circumstances, and only then after a bikeless first crossing to see if it is feasible. Almost every year someone is drowned attempting a river crossing that should never have been tried. Always ask yourself could this dilemma have been avoided in the first place by more careful planning, surely scrutiny of the proposed route would have shown that river crossings were part of the undertaking, and the weather forecast should have predicted either rain or a thaw which could be the cause of your present problem. A third possible element could be the release of water from a hydroelectric scheme which may take you by surprise in summer but will probably have less effect in winter when the water levels will probably be higher in any case.

The hydro release in summer normally has a regular pattern, eg Wednesday morning until Thursday evening on the River Garry in

This is Hazon ford, near Alnwick, Northumberland, in spate where the force of the water has eroded the bed of the crossing, so in addition to the obvious danger of a huge volume of water, conditions underfoot are hazardous too

Inverness-shire, and as part of your planning an enquiry at the local hydroelectric plant, estate office, or hotel where fishing permits are issued will provide the information you require.

If the crossing looks difficult in any way consider a detour, but also consider what such action would entail. How close is the next bridge? Is it really feasible to get there with a bike? Are the smaller burns rising too? It is amazing how quickly the lesser watercourses come into spate,

but by the same token they recede quickly too, so can you afford the time to wait, or have you sufficient protection from the elements to do so? If you have a tent erect it, get inside and have a brew, and two hours later the situation may have eased considerably.

If the terrain looks favourable move upstream to attempt the crossing, the river will eventually become smaller in that direction, and might even split into two which could be a help; but bankside

progress with a bike is never easy. Have a hard look at the map, it may be possible to retrace and attack the situation further upstream, but it is more likely that the next bridge will be downstream. Fording is seldom imperative in Britain, and in the Alps, Himalaya or even Africa, the rivers likely to destroy bridges have probably done it several times before and the locals will be the best folk to advise you on the appropriate action, like getting you to stay to assist with the rebuild!

A flying Graeme Purdy at Greensidehill Burn, Northumberland using the bike as support for leaping the stream. Don't forget to hang on and drag it across after you when you try it!

If you encounter a smaller watercourse that is too deep to ride and just too wide to leap, use your bike as a mid-stream support. Plant it nose on to the current then use it as a vaulting horse, remembering to hang onto it in the process to pull it out the far side. This technique can also be used at huge peaty pools, but beware those with soft bottoms, the bike will sink in and you could do damage to your arm trying to pull it out in one flowing movement.

Water assessment

Not all river crossings are a matter of life or death, most are more a matter of wet or dry. The natural attitude is to attempt to stay dry, and where the rocks are protruding from the water it is often possible to use the bike for extra support as you hop from stone to stone, but again watch out for the green mossy ones in summer, and those with glazed icy fringes in winter. Wet feet are

nothing when compared to a broken ankle or a fractured elbow.

The old rough stuffer's trick is to carry a spare pair of old shoes for river crossings, which isn't a bad idea, particularly in winter, although the best laid plans can have their failures. Malcolm Williams and I set out on a 39-mile winter loop linking Northumberland, Cumbria and Roxburgh, 88% of it off-road, in the knowledge that it had three river crossings, so I insisted on spare shoes. In the event all the rivers

Dry Walkers will fit over your boots, weigh about 8 ounces (227 grams), but everything has its limits. They tie just below the knee, so are really only effective to Wellington height

The line of this ford at Upper Coquetdale, Northumberland, is obvious but there is still, deep water upstream, and if you look hard enough you will see that there is a stronger current at the far bank which could well indicate deeper water, and it does!

The 'V' of the river shows where the most powerful current is — it should be obvious, but the still water beyond is often very deep

Turbulent but comparatively shallow water. Loose stones are always a potential hazard in this sort of situation, and this is the type of bottom that will induce a wavy surface when the river is in spate

Potted rules for river crossings

- Choose the safest site away from tree branches or any apparent debris
- Keep your boots on, they will provide a much firmer foothold and also protect your feet from disturbed stones and debris
- Take off your socks and keep them dry in your sack if you don't possess Dry Walkers
- If you have gaiters put them back on too, they will keep you a little warmer as well as protecting your lower legs and keeping gravel out of your boots
- Shed as much clothing as you can tolerate, put it in your sack to keep dry, preferably in sealed polythene bags within the sack, and seal the top of the bag as tightly as you can
- Keep your rucksack on but don't fasten the waistbelt, so you can shed it quickly if you fall, but try to hang onto it because it will float and provide an instant life raft
- Don't try to fight the current, move downstream sideways by cutting diagonally across. In very slow moving or still water use the bike for support facing upstream, which is always better because the force of the current may cause your knees to buckle
- Any problems, abandon the bike
- In fast water the current will push the bike towards you if you attempt to place it upstream, either carry it totally out of the water on your downstream shoulder, or keep planting it ahead of you presenting as little resistance to the current as possible, and using it as a support as you make your way to the far bank. The reason for carrying the bike on your downstream shoulder is that in the event of a fall you will probably totter downstream and fall on top of the bike, which is infinitely better than than it falling on top of you
- Inflate your spare inner tube and wear it! Honest I know someone that did it. Nice one Norman!

were frozen and we never needed them, but I'm still insisting they would have saved us a lot of discomfort under normal circumstances. Since the invention of Dry Walkers which weigh about 8 ounces, compared to the average pair of trainers which weigh about 22, you can retain dry feet for very little weight penalty, and very little loss of grip.

Once you decide the river must be crossed take a little time to find the best crossing point. Invariably everyone wants to get on with it, but check it out as far as possible, don't just plunge in, literally.

If the water is clear you will be able to assess the situation far better, possibly simply by sight. If you have polarising sunglasses or shades put them on as the fishermen do to cut out the reflected light. If the water is coloured the problem is greater, you must rely on the water surface for clues.

Wildly broken water is totally out of the question. The main flow is usually indicated by a 'V' of the smoothest water pointing downstream, this is where the current will be strongest. Large standing waves re-occurring in the same place indicate a very uneven bottom, and the famous expression 'still waters run deep' holds very true.

If there are very large rocks there could be dangerous eddies behind them, and the base of shelves or weirs always have 'stoppers' or vertical eddies below them which are to be avoided at all costs.

Often rivers become very shallow where they enter lakes, dropping their sand as they are slowed, it can often be worth checking out.

Take great care to avoid underwater obstructions, trees, broken bridges, discarded ironwork and machinery.

The upstream side of a ford is more likely to provide a suitable crossing, the downstream sides are often eroded and broken due to the fall in level and the natural increase in speed of the water.

Preparation

Choose a crossing site with easy access and exit. Avoid high banks and be aware that the outside bends always carry the deepest water, and have banks that may be undercut.

Make sure everyone knows what is going on, and if possible post 'catchers' downstream in a safe spot.

Loose clothing, particularly on your legs, should be shed because of its drag factor, but keep your boots or shoes on. They will enable you to put your feet down without fear of cuts or damage, give you better purchase, and make the crossing potentially a lot safer.

In summer you can tolerate wet clothing better than in winter, but in either season keep as much as dry as possible by taking it off and stowing it in your rucksack. The benefits of putting it back on are enormous, and have something to eat or drink after the crossing. A hot drink is wonderful regardless of the season.

In the direst of situations, or when non-swimmers are involved, help one another by doing a two- or three-person crossing with only one bike. Obviously this will involve all of you being in the water for a long time in order to get all the bikes across the river, but it might be safest. Warm up immediately the job is complete.

Remove panniers and carry them across separately. Apart from the additional weight to manoeuvre they present a large surface area to the water and can make the bike much more difficult to control.

Detouring or retracing is always preferable to a river crossing.

Chapter 9
On the trail

Planning expeditions

What is the idea behind your expedition, is it a two day epic designed to extend you or simply a means of getting into a new area, of seeing new places and new hills? Or is it the big one, a major undertaking that will last for weeks, months or even years? Most of us don't have the time to undertake the majors, our two or three week holiday is the one opportunity a year when we get the chance to really extend our experience.

Most text books will say start small and work your way up to the big one, but loads of people buy a bike and a rucksack and off they go, and often have a great time. There are odd ones that hate it or have disasters, but expeditioning is a huge learning process, that's why so many people do it again and again. It is different every time.

Try to find out as much as you can about the places you are going,

or would like to go. It adds greatly to the enjoyment. Obviously the map will show you the way, but it can also give a great deal of other information about ancient sites, the names of surrounding peaks, tracks you were not aware of, and the all important telephone symbol just in case things go awry. If you are going somewhere far off that is totally new to you read as many recent travel books and magazine articles as possible. The world changes at an amazing pace these days, and what may have been an idyllic holiday destination last year could be a no go area today. If you propose to go anywhere you are not 100% sure about get in touch with the Foreign Office (tel: 071 270 2063). They will advise you of the situation in the country you intend to visit, please heed their advice!

Just because you've got a mountain bike doesn't mean you've got to ride over mountains all the time. They make splendid touring machines, the more upright position

is easier on your back for long days in the saddle, the cantilever brakes are more powerful than side pull callipers, a factor you will appreciate when fully laden, and the fatter tyres are more comfortable and less prone to punctures. In two separate weeks on the Isle of Skye I saw only two conventional drop handlebar tourers, everyone else was riding mountain bikes, and functioning very well indeed. They also have the advantage that if you fancy a day off-road by way of a change, you have the steed.

Pure mountain bike guidebooks are on the increase, but the conventional sources such as the Shell Guides, Fodor's Blue Guides to every European country, walkers and ramblers guides, and the Great Walks books, can all give you ideas and background information to help or inspire you to plan an expedition. Spend an hour at the local library and see what fires your imagination.

Once you've got the germ of an idea get in touch with the local or national tourist office. Any Tourist Information Office will be able to give you a booklet entitled Tourist Information Centres in Britain which lists them all, and either your local Lunn Poly or the local library will supply details of the national tourist offices.

Armed with a growing mound of information you can now plan a route. This is a major part of the enjoyment. It might work, it might not work, the timetable you sketch out might be generous or it might become impossible to adhere to. I manage, more or less, to adhere to times or routes for a couple of days but beyond that I've never completed exactly what I've planned despite some horrendous epics. Maybe I'm too sociable, (pubs and rifugios seem to be a major timetable destroyer!) or too easily distracted by greater challenges. You should do better, but it's great to start with a plan, a basis for an expedition. A friend of mine, John Chambers, a chef of some distinction, set out on a tour of Europe, mainly the high and difficult bits, which turned into a tour of the pastry shops of Europe. He's one of the few people I've ever met who actually put on weight on tour, he even got as far as apportioning his money with a cake allowance for each day, didn't do half he had intended, but had an absolutely splendid time. Go with a plan but be prepared to be flexible.

Duration

What do you call an expedition? It is fair to assume that any journey involving an overnight stay is an expedition, in fact single night stopovers or weekends away arriving at your start point on the Friday night are an excellent way to begin your expeditioning career. Once you become proficient, develop a routine, you will extend it.

The next decision is where you are going to stay overnight. There is no doubt that camping provides the most flexible system, more or less stop where you drop and pitch the tent, but it is not that simple anymore. There is a complete section on camping later in the chapter. The alternatives to being under canvas are bothies, shelters and bivvies.

Bothies used to be a uniquely Scottish institution, free, simple but weatherproof buildings which eliminate the need to carry a tent, but you still need everything else - sleeping bag and cooking equipment. There are now also a few in the north of England. Although well known among bothy rats their locations are usually secret and quite often you come across them by chance. They are usually unsupervised but each has been adopted either by a section of the Mountain Bothies Association (MBA) or a mountaineering organisation.

Unfortunately they suffer a lot of damage, usually at the hands of a minority of their users foraging for firewood, which is a disgrace, the stalwarts of the MBA must despair at times. Some of the better known buildings now appear on Ordnance Survey maps simply as 'bothy', but you may get a nasty shock. The building at 19/838665 in Shieldaig Forest, Wester Ross, turned out to be a burned out shell when we reached it one saturated October day, so keep as up to date as you can.

Shelters and emergency bivouacs or bivvies, are even simpler, smaller and more secret than the bothies, although here again they are starting to appear on the map. They vary from rough dry stone beehives to tiny lays roofed with corrugated iron and turf which may be passed by unnoticed. They are what they say, emergency shelters and shouldn't be relied upon as accommodation.

The easiest and most productive in terms of distance is using bed and breakfast facilities, either the usual B&Bs or even hotels. The immediate disadvantage is cost, but there is no doubt a good shower and a good bed will sustain you longer than a windswept, rain battered night spent in cramped conditions. The greatest advantage of B&B is the ability to travel light, and it's up to you how far you go in this respect. I met a small group of riders in the Dolomites who I assumed were only

Shelters are usually 'on the crude side', and really only emergency bivouac sites. This example near the Fords of Avon, Cairngorms, Scotland, is cramped, and damp, but nevertheless affords welcome relief from the elements when the need arises

Left: Tarn Beck Bothy, Cumbria, a rare English example, but one of the most comfortable

having a day out by their almost total lack of equipment, but it transpired that they were on a vehicle supported tour, hitting the passes hard, sometimes even meeting the truck for lunch, then pressing on over the next range. Their pass total for the week was impressive, and they weren't sparing the bikes on the descents, mechanical failures could be fixed at the bottom of the hill. It was probably not in the spirit of advanced mountain biking, but they had the legs on me.

What they would be lacking would be the aesthetic enjoyment of the mountains late in the day as the sun set, or first thing in the morning, or even during the night when nocturnal beasts wander by. There is much more to expeditions than simply covering the miles.

Extended expeditions

Unless you are sponsored, or supported in some way the main consideration for long expeditions will be finance. If it is undertaken as an extended holiday the answer is relatively simple, you must save up before you go. Research into the cost of living in the various places you intend to pass through will prove very interesting and no doubt provide a wealth of background knowledge. Working *en route* is another alternative, but this depends

on where you go and at what time of year. Fruit picking seems the obvious example, but some years ago that well known guitarist Tym Manley made it to India and back on £30 having played his way across Europe and a fair bit of Asia !

Prior arrangement with journals, magazines or newspapers who are willing to take accounts of your travels might be a way of financing the expedition, but you will need to be going somewhere pretty special to justify interest. If you choose to journey through the less populated and poorer countries it may be wise to send spares such as tyres, brake blocks, bottom bracket bearings, chains or rear blocks on ahead using the *Poste Restante* facilities of post offices in the biggest cities you can reach, or the similar facilities of the American Express organisation.

Obviously you would get the appropriate inoculations before leaving home but some have a limited life, so you will need to engineer your expedition to be in a place where boosters or renewals can be obtained at the appropriate time.

Serious expeditioners would be well advised to contact the Expeditionary Advisory Centre of the Royal Geographical Society (Tel: 071 589 5466) where not only will you get the best advice in the world, but will be able to purchase excellent specific literature among

which *Expedition Medicine* ranks very highly.

Party size

The bigger the party the greater the chance of conflict. Decision making becomes a nightmare with several points of view and several people to consider, but a proven and well-matched partner is a good idea. You can share problems, even physically help one another through the bad times, bounce ideas around and have a laugh together, but three or more on an expedition of any length either demands a strong leader who will make all the decisions or incredible luck to stay together.

Of course there is nothing to stop half a dozen folk travelling in pairs and meeting up, but don't expect everyone to be equally matched or have the same attitude to, or expectations of what is taking place.

You meet far more people when travelling solo as you're often dying to talk to someone! That is the main disadvantage, very long trips alone can play havoc with your thought patterns which isn't always healthy. The advantages of travelling solo are no arguments about where to go, the speed of travel, diversions to take in points of interest, resting or days off. You just please yourself. The disadvantages apart from the solitude, are the dangers of taking ill alone. Having nobody to share the

Dreaming of bigger things. Get the map out. There's sure to be an old pass climbing around the big bluff

Climbing a rock can have its uses: if the trail disappears a little extra elevation might unlock the mystery

In winter larger parties of riders, six or seven, are not only more acceptable, but probably more desirable because there aren't so many other people about

load can also be a problem, although Andrew Brown and Tim Garrat took a tent each on their round the world trip, claiming their own living space was psychologically vital.

Closer to home, large parties are not always welcome in the hills. Three tends to become half a dozen, four equals ten, and if there are actually half a dozen the group assumes horde proportions in the eyes of some landowners and other hill users. However, larger parties of six or seven are not only more acceptable, but probably desirable in winter when there aren't so many people about.

In parties where there are younger members keep a close eye on them, particularly in poor conditions. They are more susceptible to mountain hypothermia, but will press on regardless rather than let you know they are having trouble with the pace.

Your timetable

The greatest shock to your expedition timetable will be your speed when heavily laden. After the first weekend away you could well become a total lightweight freak! It

109

should go without saying that you will be slower over the ground when heavily laden, but true off-roading will really eat into your time because there will be so many more stretches where you will be forced to walk not only because it is not possible to ride a laden bike, but also in the interests of gear preservation.

Carrying extra gear, no matter how little, will put extra strain on the bike and increase the possibility of mechanical failure. First-class bike preparation will help enormously, but also slowing down a little over the roughest ground will extend the life of your equipment. After all, stopping to fix a failure, or having to limp out will absorb a lot more time than merely slowing down to provide a modicum of bike sympathy.

Personal kit

No matter how dedicated you are, after three or more days, or perhaps even less, pressing on and working hard at your expedition you will need some form of relaxation. No matter how hard you have pruned your gear weight-wise, there must always be some personal item worthy of taking for the simple reason it will help you relax. A book, a walkman or even a diary are frequent companions. The veteran Saharan traveller Tony Golding recommends you take the lot, you'll need them!

Essential in many parts of Africa these days is a supply of sterile needles and the appropriate syringe to give a qualified person to use on you, and antibiotic powder for drying and disinfecting wounds is a useful addition to your first aid kit.

If you are highly disciplined all you will need to do is assemble your gear, choose a venue and a date and off you go, but the advantage of organised events is twofold: there is always an element of back up or support in case anything goes wrong, and you will see lots of other equipment used by other competitors and can compare its performance with your own. I have found the International Polaris MTB Challenge the ideal vehicle to try new, usually minimalist, ideas, and the Iditabike Challenge in Alaska really embraces the limits to the point where you need to be totally competent to take part. It works for me, it might work for you.

Kit carrying

You have three options for the manner of carrying your gear when mountain biking. The first is to carry it on yourself in a bumbag or rucksack, the second is to put it all into bags that are attached to your bike by various means, and the third is to develop a mix using body and bike that will suit you on the particular type of journey you are about to undertake.

The body option, carrying all your needs in a bumbag or rucksack has definite advantages, but you are limited by how much you can carry. In fact you can inflict permanent damage on your back by carrying too much over long distances over rough terrain, so be very reasonable, or even kind to yourself with this option. Try to travel as light as possible, don't buy a big rucksack because you'll fill it, restrict yourself to about 25 litres capacity. You can always add extra luggage space later by using a bumbag or bar bag. In general terms this will limit you to day rides, weekends and commuting, but you could also undertake extended tours in Europe as opposed to expeditions with this amount of kit.

The main disadvantage of carrying all your equipment, clothing and food on your bike is the fact that it alters the handling of the machine so much and makes it harder to hump over obstacles. You can detach the panniers but how many people do that during a journey? We always try to push or lift the whole lot until we are exhausted, **then** we take the bags off and resort to a double carry. With panniers and other attached bags you must always aim for spread and balance of the load. The big advantage is the fact that you can convert the bike into a total pack animal and carry enormous loads if you stick to reasonable terrain, not necessarily tarmac roads, but eliminating technical bumpy single track.

For most of us on most occasions a sensible mix of some stuff carried on your back and the rest on your bike seems appropriate. On the very first Polaris Challenge I went totally to panniers and my partner Alex Spence went totally rucksack. Neither of us fared particularly well, especially me when my ancient bags jumped off on the first downhill. We learned a lot in two days, it is a totally different ball game riding fully loaded off-road, but it seriously extends your range.

Other luggage

Build up your luggage collection as you would your apparel, gearing it to your most frequent use. You always carry tools so a little saddle pack like Trek's Basic Pack 80 or a Shoulder Holder which adds comfort when carrying will become a permanent fixture.

Day rides are most frequent. For these a bumbag or expanding bumbag will suffice, perhaps a little rucksack like Karrimor's Diddy or even a good old fashioned saddlebag by Carradice. My 'new' one is 16-years old and still going strong, has

good capacity and it won't obstruct your Sam Browne belt or reflective material on your jacket if you're caught out after dark.

You can augment these arrangements with a handlebar bag such as Vaude's Vigan or the well-established Bardale or Bardet by Karrimor who now have a totally waterproof Aquashield Bardet (as they do in the panniers) which has a canoe-type closure in case you want to spend all your holidays in Norway!

Single overnight stops or weekends away usually demand more luggage, but it depends where you intend to stay. If it is a youth hostel or bed and breakfast you've probably got enough capacity already, or you could add a top bag on a rack like Caratti's Bag Rack Pack. Camping demands a lot more and could push you into the realm of panniers, although with clever choice of kit, and sharing the load with your partner it is possible to keep the weight down to 11 or 12 pounds each and fit it all into the likes of a Karrimor KIMM Sac or a MacPac Condor.

Bumbags
Bumbags are great but they have their limitations. Originally designed for fell running and skiing they've grown in popularity and size. If you load up a bumbag with heavy objects like tools, cameras or even

water bottles you are asking a lot of the buckle, or more precisely the buckle and belt material combination, and this is where many fall down - literally. The constant pressure causes the belt to work loose. A Berghaus bumbag I owned was the worst example I've come across but I cured it by stitching matching pieces of Velcro at intervals on the tail of the belt and on the waistband, so if yours starts to fall down there is a solution. However the manufacturers choice of waistband material should preclude this.

The great advantage of a bumbag is that it limits what you can carry! So you've got to travel light and think about your kit. It also allows most of your back to breathe, a major plus in hot weather.

Some bumbags explode into mini-rucksacks and I openly admit to being a fan of this design. It suits me down to the ground. I try to limit myself to what the lower compartment will hold, but if you need to shed clothing it can be put in the top section, or in winter you can carry an extra garment in the top until you need it. The material used for the upper compartment needs to be quite thin and light otherwise it takes up most of the space in the bottom section when you tuck it away.

My favourite is made by Ellis Brigham, closely followed by

Outbound's Forme 4 which is
slightly bigger.

Rucksacks

Rucksacks are a bit like panniers in
that you need them to be as
waterproof as possible, no
unnecessary straps flapping about to
slap you in the face on the fastest
part of a downhill, and be nice and
secure when you are moving. If you
go beyond the 25-litre capacity a
waiststrap is essential and a chest
strap a good bonus. Unlike walkers
we are constantly leaping about and
occasionally flying so you must have
a stable load.

   My favourites are the KIMM Sac
and the MacPac Ultramarathon.
Karrimor's 30-litre KIMM Sac
developed as its name suggests from
their long association with the
Karrimor International Mountain
Marathon. This is an ultra-
lightweight sac designed to carry
enough for the overnight camp on
the mountain marathon and is ideal
for mountain biking. It has no less
than seven outside pockets, mainly
of mesh, so given the right weather
and crafty use you can actually dry
things as you ride along. The two in
the waist wings are big enough to
accept nutrition bars so you can eat
on the move. It doesn't have any
sort of frame so you've got to pack
it carefully, but the bag itself only
weighs 300g and the lattice
compression cord is a great system

Top: The Karrimor KIMM Sac, was
originally designed for the Karrimor
Mountain Marathon, as the name suggests.
It's ultra lightweight and ideal for mountain
biking when packed correctly

MacPac Ultramarathon. Another bag
spawned by competition, more like a super
bumbag, with great stability achieved by
four-way harness adjustment, it even has
side holsters for water bottles (or fruit on
the run) and a built in sleeping mat big
enough to insulate your back

for making a solid lump of your load
even if it is only half full. It's an
action sac with a pedigree and for
my money the best bag available.

   The MacPac Ultramarathon, 22
litres, is a concept sac aimed at total
comfort on the move and is totally
adjustable. It can be moulded to
your body shape using the shoulder
straps, chest brace, waistbelt and the
side compression straps. It has its
own built in sleeping mat which is
great as a lunchtime seat but I have
reservations about it as a bed in all
but the warmest weather. Ladies
might not like the positioning of the
chest brace, but you don't have to
use it.

Panniers and racks

One serious expeditioner told me
that he believed the totally
waterproof pannier hadn't been
invented until Karrimor introduced
their canoe-type closures on the tops
of their Aquashield range.

   In all fairness most panniers are
99% waterproof when they are new
and it is only commonsense to wrap
perishables and dry clothing in plastic
bags, giving extra proofing.
Manufacturers have gone to
extraordinary lengths to produce
satisfactory bags, even thread that
swells when it is wet because the
holes made by sewing are the weak
point in pannier manufacture. Some
come with supplementary waterproof
covers, or you can buy your own.

Make sure your sac is properly adjusted. A good quality, well-fitting sac is essential for comfortable days out in the hills. This lad, spotted on the Passo di Limo high in the Dolomites, expends so much effort balancing or compensating for his bag, that his bike handling suffers accordingly

A variety of materials are used in pannier construction from the heavy tightly woven Cotton Duck which is undoubtedly one of the hardest wearing materials available, through the excellent Cordura and heavy-weight nylons to very lightweight proofed nylon. As ever you must make the difficult choices between cost, weight and durability. Anticipate the intended use and the frequency, because most panniers are used only once or twice a year, but as always you only get what you pay for. What to look for:

Hooks and fastenings Make sure that the panniers will be secure on the rack, for off-road use they need a clip like Karrimor's Secura-lock (SL) which has a secondary spring latch to stop them jumping up and off, or a supplementary strap that allows them to be tied tightly to the rack, and a good strong lower fastening.

Lid overlap Make sure that the top lid covers the main compartment when the bag is filled to capacity.

Stiff back Soft panniers will deform after extended use, make sure each bag has a good stout back and reinforcing at the hook attachment points.

Waterproofing Despite what has already been said about waterproof qualities, the drier you can keep your kit the easier it is all round. Make sure any zips have flaps to limit the ingress of water.

Tidy straps Make sure that straps cannot flap into the spokes when the panniers are only half full or empty.

Desirable features include:

Reflective material Some manufacturers use these in their name tag.

Carrying handle Useful if you are carrying more than one.

Reinforcements In high-wear areas like the bottom of the backs where they touch the frame mounting.

Screw-on hooks For easier replacement.

Ties To fasten both panniers together for airline transport, they are less likely to lose a big lump.

Getting the best out of your panniers

Keep them clean and dry! They will collect a lot of dirt off-road, clean them and hang them up to dry. If they seem to be losing their waterproof qualities spray them with Grangers Super Pel. Seams can be treated with tent sealant.

Recommended panniers are Karrimor Kalahari 3, the 26-litre capacity per pair is just about the maximum for truly off-road expeditions. Excellent SL locking clips stop them jumping up and off, high-visibility lids, easy access outer net pockets, in short, well designed, well made and highly recommended.

Jack Wolfskin Unipack are also good, having an amount of reflective material on the lids, Velcro safety strap to stop them jumping off, and the capacity of 18 litres: they should be sufficient for most needs.

Vaude Front Panniers are a budget option. In reality they'll go on either the front or the back. Their capacity is 16 litres per pair, nothing fancy, durable, will probably need the added security of a bungee for peace of mind on the rougher routes. An ideal starter pack, do you need more?

Pannier racks

It is truly amazing how much can be carried on a pannier rack, in fact they lend themselves to overloading and abuse. What type of rack you choose depends on the intended use, or more honestly the country of intended use.

Cyclists automatically look at the weight of any component or accessory, but with pannier racks this is of secondary importance to good design and strength. Saving 30 or 40 grams pales into insignificance when you attach 30 or 40 litres of pannier capacity and then fill them up. Having said this it is not obligatory to attach panniers, you can use a top bag or a tunnel bag enclosed by your sleeping mat, fastened on with straps, or my favourite, bungees. If you've ever carried your sleeping mat on the top of your rucksack on the bike you'll appreciate the linear streamlining you achieve by tying it on a rack. They are worth it for that alone.

The fear with aluminium alloy racks is that if they break you stand little or no chance of getting them welded. However, ultra-long-distance traveller Sally Millard has had her faithful Blackburn seven years now and it has seen service in Sri Lanka, most of India and the Himalaya, and looks as if it will do another seven, but, and it's a big but, experienced expeditioner Tony Golding's front rack broke without warning on the second day of an Icelandic tour, having seen service in Europe and twice across the Sahara. (Why would anyone want to cross the Sahara **twice?**) It could have received rough treatment at the hands of baggage handlers which is something you must consider. My son Graeme even had the experience of seeing his bike bumping up the escalator with cases and other luggage and dropping out onto the carousel in Crete, fortunately without too much damage, and apparently this is not too unusual. I must have been lucky so far.

The advantage of aluminium racks is their weight. Trek's tubular Backrack weighs in at 530g exactly the same as the Blackburn mountain bike rack which is made from solid aluminium rod. The choice is yours. Tubular aluminium is claimed to be stronger than rod, you can usually tell by looking. In the solid rod department there are many Blackburn lookalikes but only time will tell if they will perform as well for so long.

The best steel racks are tubular, most using hydraulic tubing which is strong and light, but whichever you choose it must fit the bike. Most racks fit most bikes, but if you have a small frame you may encounter difficulty, so check sizes before you buy. Racks must be mounted with the top platform and top side support rails which take the pannier hooks level, otherwise the bags will slide forwards and catch your heels, or backwards and have you pulling wheelies all the way to your destination.

The wheelie is a common problem in off-road situations. Often folk can only afford rear

panniers which are the usual initial purchase, load them up for a tour then find they can't keep the front wheel on the ground on bumpy stretches. It is obviously an extra expense but try to maintain the balance of the bike by carrying some of the load on the front in either panniers or a bar bag, which brings us to the choice of front pannier racks.

The low rider style of rack is very popular with road tourers, it keeps your centre of gravity low and helps with stability, but for off-road use they have two disadvantages. They are right down in the mud and water, and can catch on rocks or the side of the track. The answer is to use a normal height carrier or even a top bag on the platform, provided it doesn't obstruct your view.

Potential problems

Front carriers and racks are more susceptible to coming loose due to vibration and flexing of the forks. Use either Nylok or checknuts (two nuts) to secure the bolts, even if they have been inserted through screwed brazed on bosses. Nylok nuts are a patented design initially used in the aircraft industry, they have a nylon insert on the outward side of the nut which grips the thread of the bolt tightly, and are well worth using at the rear and when attaching

mudguards too. The universal size for bolts and bosses is 5mm.

If you are buying another bike look for brazed on bosses. The Specialised range fare best in this department.

The problem with wheelies has already been mentioned, but also bear in mind that when your rear wheel already carries most of your bodyweight your additional baggage could well cause problems. Some really serious expeditioners go as far as having 48-spoke wheels built, a 25% increase on your average mountain bike wheel, and even then they carry a spare spoke or two. Put the lighter but bulky stuff in the rear panniers.

If you intend using the largest pannier bags get a rack with a deep framework to prevent the corners of the panniers swinging, or being knocked into the wheels.

If a rack does break all is not lost, be prepared to improvise.

The simplest repairs are invariably splints secured with wire. You can use your spare spokes; a broken rack can be splinted with two 10mm spanners bound with fencing wire; or try strong string and sticky tape in a real emergency. Load redistribution to favour the broken rack will also help.

Final word concerns the nighthawks. The rear rack is a great place to mount your back light, it's central so you've no worries which side of the road you're riding on! and if it's not sticking out to the side it will not be bashed so often.

Locks

Taking a lock on any expedition is worthwhile. In the vast majority of places it will not be needed, but mountain bikes are objects of desire worldwide, particularly if you are alone, and the reassurance your lock will provide makes it worth carrying.

Thieves are not so likely to come equipped with bolt croppers and power saws in the wilder places, although they might shoot the lock off wild west style on the Khyber Pass, so a cable lock seems best. A good long cable will allow you to tie the bike to trees, thread it through walls and around gateposts, and might even encompass your panniers. They are highly favoured by long distance expeditionists. The alternative is an ultra-light D lock.

Self sufficiency

The well-prepared mountain biker will always be self sufficient. Your tool kit will reflect your level of preparation, but depending on where you are going you might want to take a few extras.

It is amazing how quickly bike shops die off as you leave the cities, and whereas a garage or agricultural workshop might be able to cobble up or manufacture a repair to get you home, they won't have the specialised tools needed to strip the likes of a freewheel.

A freewheel remover is a useful addition and a spare set of cables useful insurance. Your elastoplast will double as sticky tape, but you might want to back it up with copper wire and epoxy resin of some sort. You can even fabricate bits out of wood with your Swiss army knife when pushed!

Camping

The big advantages of camping are that it gives the greatest flexibility of travel, overnight accommodation, and timetabling. Within reason, and subject to the laws of the country where you find yourself, you can stop and sleep just about anywhere. There is no searching for a bed at the end of the day, you've got it with you, and if you need an obscenely early start or you might not finish until really late, there are no problems. However, if you are using an official site keep your noise down, tents provide next to nothing in the way of sound insulation.

The disadvantage of camping is that you've got to carry your house, bed and kitchen with you. If there are two of you the load can be shared, which helps, but if you are on your own you've got to carry the lot.

The extra burden of camping equipment will affect the handling of the bike and slow you down. Allow for this in your timetable. There is no point in carrying so much kit that you are never going to reach the idyllic destination that might be afforded by camping. Think light.

Routine

Inasmuch as camping is an exercise in freedom you'll find yourself developing a routine, often dictated by the weather. In cold weather you will often light the stove first for a hot brew before starting to pitch the tent. If it is raining the tent will go up first, and again the tent will take precedence if it is blowing a gale because you'll want, or need, to cook in the porch. In either case the tent and cooking equipment are top of the list, so pack them so you can set up as soon as you stop.

Many chores take longer when camping so allow for this in your timetable. Cold frosty mornings can absorb as much as two hours from waking to rolling. At the other end of the day it doesn't seem to matter how long is spent over the evening meal, the odds are that you will probably only go for a short walk after it then turn in for the night.

A selection of medium sized geodesics, used as base camp for the Polaris Challenge

Tents

If you are new to camping choosing a tent must be a baffling task, there are so many shapes, weights and colours. Again it comes down to intended use. There are three basic types, valley tents, mountain tents and all-year-round four season tents. Within these categories there are five different basic designs, the original ridge tent, single hoop, tunnel, dome and geodesic.

Official campsites are usually located in low level valleys, are flat, well drained and quite well protected. There will be toilet facilities, showers, a shop and perhaps even a pub. Some also have drying facilities which can be expedition savers. If you intend to use these sites you can capitalise on the benefits and buy a really small lightweight tent, such as a single hoop or sloping ridge, not worrying about size because with all the facilities near at hand you're not likely to be cooped up in there for any length of time. Weights for a two person tent will vary from 1.9kg to 4kg.

Mountain tents demand a greater decision, and your choice will be further complicated by trying to decide whether you will be using the tent as a base within the mountains or lugging it day after day. If it rains in the mountains you could be confined to your tent for hours so you need more room. Your campsite will not be a manicured stone-free pitch, and you'll have to take what comes in the way of lumps and bumps, so the tent needs to be that bit tougher, and capable of being firmly secured down to withstand high winds. Weight might rise a little but you should be able to keep a two person tent down to 4kg.

Ridge and geodesic designs with valances have the advantage that rocks can be used to weight them down and provide extra stability. Tunnel tents are usually very spacious but need to be pitched tail into the wind, although the most advanced models have entrances at both ends so if the wind changes it is no problem. Dome and geodesic designs are particularly suitable for mountain sites, being able to withstand winds from any direction.

Winter nights are long so your four-season tent needs plenty of room both to live in, and store your wet gear out of the way. The weather could be severe so good guying and an ample valance are prerequisites. Weight could rise to 5kg.

A geodesic this size brings a weight penalty, which you might not be prepared to accept in the summer, but the extra space afforded could be worth its weight in gold on long winter nights, or when entombed by bad weather

Size

Size is important, too many people buy a really tiny tunnel tent to make maximum saving on weight, run into wet weather, then find they can't even sit up in it. The average person requires an internal height of at least 95cm to be comfortable, but if you are over six-feet tall you may want more. The length of mountain tents isn't usually a problem but again check out the length of the sleeping area if you are very tall. The size of the porch or vestibule will dictate how much gear can be stored there and how much room you have for cooking. Tents with two entrances not only give you the option of the best cooking area but extra room for stowing kit.

Groundsheets should always be substantial. You do a lot of kneeling in a tent which tests groundsheet waterproof qualities to the limit, and jagged stones can be a problem. If possible provide protection by laying something else down first, a survival bag, piece of polythene or even a supplementary groundsheet. This will also keep the groundsheet clean and remove the necessity of wiping the base before moving on.

Tent pegs

Most tents come with light alloy pegs which are excellent in soft ground, the scooped shape taking a lot more lateral force than the skewer type. For rocky sites something more substantial is needed to withstand

Typical peg weights

	Length	Weight
Plastic (Hamptons)	31cm	28g
Plastic (Hamptons)	20cm	16g
Scooped aluminium (MacPac)	17cm	22g
Steel - straight	17cm	28.6g
Twisted steel	16cm	17g
Aluminium alloy - straight (Hamptons)	16cm	17g
Steel - straight	13cm	14.5g

being driven in with a rock. Straight or twisted steel pegs or the specially toughened straight aluminium alloy pattern made by the Hampton Works of Birmingham are easier to place between the stones. Heavy duty plastic pegs are increasingly popular for the major guys (if your tent has them) despite their bulk they are very light, but many plastics break in sub zero temperatures.

Pegs always seem an area where weight can be saved, but there isn't that much between them. The best plan is to carry a mixture suited to the terrain and save weight on the overall length.

Wilderness camping

Wilderness is relative. It could be a corner of your garden allowed to go wild, it could be open country only a few miles from the edge of an industrial connurbation, or it could be the never ending Siberian taiga. No doubt your perception of wilderness will become remoter and wilder with time and experience, but for most of us it is somewhere different from our usual environment, somewhere demanding considerable effort to reach, but somewhere well worth visiting. If we are not careful we could love the place to death. We must all strive to cause as little disturbance and damage to these environments as possible, to let later visitors appreciate what we have enjoyed.

The extreme attitude could be don't go at all, any visitation will cause a degree of change, a degree of erosion no matter how small, so the only way is to stay away. This is a personal decision, and certainly some environments should be left undisturbed, but we are learning all the time and with consideration and practise our passing should go virtually undetected and our enjoyment all the more for that.

My attitude to what is acceptable camping practice has been refined over the years, I hope I have become more environmentally friendly. We have a tremendous responsibility to set a good example and hopefully leave our own particular wilderness unchanged so that we can return in years hence and repeat the experience.

Choosing the location

A level site to pitch your tent is essential if you don't want complications during the night. A sloping site will have you rolling down the hill in your slumbers and finishing up in a huddle in one corner of the tent. It also makes cooking on a stove easier and safer, with less likelihood of spillage.

Try to find a stone free and well-drained spot. All too often level sites are damp too, and try not to pitch near a noisy mountain stream if you want an undisturbed night's rest. Water courses coming quickly into spate due to heavy rain must also be considered, it is amazing how quickly mountain streams and becks can rise, never underestimate them.

Plenty of room is highly desirable, somewhere to stand or lie the bikes where they don't interfere with camp chores, and if frost is expected keep out of hollows where the coldest air sinks at night. Have a walk round, check out the vicinity for hazards before it gets dark. Look for barbed wire, crags, ravines, old mine workings and deep water, and pass the information on to others.

Don't camp too close to the base of crags, stonefall is the obvious danger but I also heard of someone who had a sheep fall down onto the tent during the night, fortunately they survived much better than the flying ovine.

Protection

When pitching your tent allow for the 'worse case' scenario. Point the door away from the wind so that you don't end up living in a balloon. On difficult sites you can weigh down the pegs with rocks but keep them off the guys, a night's wind can fray them through.

Take advantage of any natural protection on the site: try to put trees or hillocks between you and the wind. Camping under trees might give you initial protection from the rain but the droplets forming in the trees usually become

bigger than raindrops and as a result have a greater chance of penetrating your flysheet.

Protection from animals is also worthy of consideration. In the UK the greatest problem is likely to be cattle or sheep, or a marauding fox, but in North America bears can be a serious threat. Keep all foodstuffs inside the tent, unless you're in bear country then you've got to hang it up a tree, but rumour has it that yetis love Mars bars and termites eat your shoes. You have been warned.

The view

One of the primary reasons for getting out there is the view. You may forget the difficulties of the day's journey as time passes, but you always remember the campsites, so why not try for a site with the best view and drink in the atmosphere. Perfect campsites are found not made, so if you find one before the intended end of your day why not just stop there for the night, it will be worth it.

Most of us seek seclusion, or at least only the company of our chosen travelling companions. We are more likely to tolerate the

company of strangers on the trail than at the overnight camp. The later in the day you make camp the more likely you are to achieve this, and the further you are from civilisation the greater your chances of success.

Choosing your site

There is a school of thought that

suggests that everyone should find a new campsite, use it very carefully, and leave it as they found it. Then the impact of camping would be lessened and barely noticeable. The only problem is that in more remote countryside, or even in highly desirable locations such as lakesides,

Far Left: Go straight through the middle of muddy tracks to avoid doing more damage to the area. It is seldom the easiest route, but no one said conservation was easy

Left: It is essential to stick to established tracks in sandy areas, veering off in search of grip could be absolutely disastrous for the struggling plant life

Green Cleuch, Pentland Hills, Midlothian, Scotland is in need of conservation. This is a long established way through the Hills, and it's not difficult to see why mountain bikers are getting the blame for the current erosion. The Edinburgh mountain bikers, guided by the Pentland Park Rangers, organised a work party to repair the damage

certain spots are everyone's ideal campsite so they get used over and over again.

We could say 'Don't camp by the lakeside despite it being the most desirable place, move back a couple of hundred metres.' Then when you've pitched your tent on a second-class site, someone else comes along and camps at the lakeside. What is the answer, do you go down and throw them in?

Some sites are always popular. They get hammered with use, erosion is evident, vegetation shrinks back. Why not continue to use them, the damage has already been done. Is it not better to use a high impact site than to start another somewhere else? In some places this might be the kindest, and most convenient thing to do.

There is a difficult dilemma when choosing a campsite. What is the location that will cause least damage to the environment we have travelled so far to enjoy? Arguably the most durable campsite would be on rock. That's OK but how do you anchor the tent? Initially the effects of camping can seem insignificant, some minor trampling of vegetation, blackening of a few stones used to build a fire ring, or a little less firewood close to camp. With more use it gets worse, vegetation disappears, then erosion sets in, tree roots are exposed, then surface water runoff creates its own erosion, and we have a serious problem.

The most durable sites are usually those which can regenerate or renew themselves easily. Gravel or sand won't take much harm, and using gravel pits near rivers will have the bonus that even your footprint disturbance will be obliterated by the next flood, but of course you have the noise and rising water factors to consider. Pine forest floors often have a good covering of litter or duff which not only suffers little harm but is comfortable to lie on. Of course fires are strictly taboo in these situations.

Snow and ice are periodically removed by the natural cycle, but by far the best is dry tough grass. Grass provides a cushioning effect and its roots keep the soil particles bound together. You may have a visual impact camping out in the open on a meadow or moor, but a couple of

days after you've left the grass will have recovered.

Fires

Many keen conservationists talk about kicking the habit as far as open fires are concerned, and in the UK there has been a tremendous swing towards stoves in the last 10 years, not least because wood near high impact sites has become difficult to obtain.

The question arises are fires acceptable at all. The easy answer is NO, but for many folk a camp fire is part and parcel of the whole exercise despite the fact that the cooking can be haphazard and the pots difficult to clean. Fires can also be the deciding factor whether you may be tolerated in a certain area, or chased off.

If you find a site where there is already a fire ring, use it, don't create a new one. Small as it is, damage has already been done, so settle for that.

If you use a pristine site and must have a fire build one on a mound of earth or in a pit, avoiding vegetated areas. If there is no option than to site your fire in a vegetated area, remove the litter or vegetation in such a manner that it can be replaced. Scrape a shallow pit several centimetres deep and build your fire inside. A wide pit minimises the risk of spread of fire but there is no need to fill it with flames, build your fire

no larger than necessary.

Gather dead wood for your fire, riversides are usually good for this, never chop down trees. When you are finished with the fire cool the ash and the surrounding soil with water if necessary, then fill the pit with the excavated soil, replace your vegetation and camouflage the site with natural leaf litter. It all sounds a bit of a performance. It is much quicker, more environmentally acceptable, and easier to use a stove.

Sleeping bags

Some sleeping bags use natural down and feathers as insulation, others use synthetics. Down has more loft and warmth for lower weight and volume and lasts well, but is useless when wet. Synthetics stay warm when wet, are cheaper, but for the same warmth are considerably heavier and bulkier.

Regardless of the type of filling, sleeping bags rely on the ability to trap air for their insulation. The greater the loft, or thickness of insulation, the more air is trapped, the warmer the bag. Down and feathers recover their natural shape very well when unpacked but are very expensive, similar levels of loft can be achieved by the synthetics but there is a substantial bulk and weight penalty. Under compression the air is expelled and you are left with a pretty thin layer of insulating material, which is a good characteristic from a packing point of view, but no good for keeping warm. MacPac took the bold step of dispensing with the down filling on the back of their super lightweight Pinnacle bag altogether, replacing it with a pocket into which you slip your sleeping mat, so even if you roll over in the night the mat goes with you; but this is a specialist bag and it would be a bold camper that committed themselves to prolonged use in the depths of winter.

Many synthetic fillings are attached to the cover material, but loose fillings such as down will 'migrate' and allow cold spots to form if the bag is not constructed properly. This is usually achieved by creating compartments by way of overlapping box quilting ensuring that there is no stitching through both surfaces of the bag. Zips can cause cold spots so choose a bag with draught baffles behind them. Hoods or cowls are strongly recommended, otherwise you'll need a hat.

Sleeping bag jargon relating to performance is usually quoted in 'seasons'. The table should clarify suitability and recommended use, but as conditions in the valley and on the hill vary considerably so you must adjust your sleeping bag requirements accordingly.

Sleeping mats

A sleeping bag can never provide total insulation from the ground, in fact there can be serious heat loss through conduction while you sleep. A separate sleeping mat, air bed or mattress is a necessity. Mattresses are inordinately bulky, air beds tend to be extremely heavy, so the answer lies with the sleeping mat.

Much progress has been made since the first Karrimats appeared, and the originals are still first class, but even they come in two specifications and three thicknesses. Again intended use rears its head but basically the thicker the mat the more insulation provided, it comes down to how big a roll you are prepared to carry.

Stoves and safety

There are four means of boiling your water and heating your food without building a fire, gas, pressure stoves, meths burners and solid block fuel.

Gas is clean requires no preliminaries or maintenance, just turn it on and light it. It's quite expensive to run. Low temperature and high altitude burning problems have been overcome by EPIgas with their butane/propane mix, and you can limit your pack weight by choosing the appropriate self-sealing safety cartridge for that particular expedition.

Pressure stoves usually require cleaning, priming and occasional pricking, but having said this they are cheap to run and the fuel is readily available throughout the world. Petrol stoves have the reputation of being more volatile than their paraffin counterparts, but properly used and controlled work very well indeed. The Highland guru, Norman Brett, uses a petrol stove exclusively: 'Because on lonely Highland nights you need some sort of company, and the petrol stove gurgles, spits, and talks back.'

Meths burners are simple, safe and super reliable. Their only very minor drawback is the fact that they burn quietly and the flame is nearly invisible, especially in bright sun. They have no moving parts, perform well in windy conditions and are very easy to use. The Trangia is the best known, and an excellent performer.

	Mountain	Valley
One season	summer & specialist eg Polaris Challenge	late spring, summer, early autumn
Two season	late spring, summer, early autumn	spring, summer, autumn
Three season	spring, summer, autumn	winter
Four season	winter	winter

Solid methylated fuel blocks such as Meta or Carricook provide arguably the lightest means of heating, the tiny military style burners are undoubtedly the lightest, but they provide a slow heat. On most occasions this doesn't matter, but sometimes it can be infuriating.

With all stoves there is some danger of setting the tent alight when cooking indoors, and there are also the fumes to consider. If it is not possible to cook outside ensure a firm level base and adequate ventilation. Gas is heavier than air, a leaking appliance could easily inundate the tent up to the height of the sewn-in groundsheet overnight. Store stoves and cartridges in the vestibule or outside altogether.

Take great care with boiling water or hot food. It is so easy to trip over guys or other kit when concentrating on supper. (Have you ever tried picking a pan of cooked pasta shells out of long grass? It is hopeless!)

Hygiene

Water is the major prerequisite of any campsite. Water for cooking and water for washing. At one time the advice would have been gather your drinking water above your camp and do your washing below. This is probably OK for you, but what about others downstream, we must consider them.

Gather water from an unpolluted source. If you are not perfectly satisfied that it is pollution free it must be either sterilised, usually with tablets or boiled, or filtered. Tablets taste the water; boiling uses up fuel, but most of the things you will be eating involve boiling water, so it's not a waste of resources. Filters are very expensive but absolutely essential for third world expeditions.

Don't forget your personal hygiene. Wash all your utensils in hot water if it is at all possible, and wash your hands before eating. There is no point in having sterile food if you don't wash hands that have just freed off brakes jammed with moorland dross.

In an effort to keep the streams as pure as possible do your washing some distance away from the stream, this will give the ground a chance to filter your waste water before it re-enters the watercourse. In the unlikely event of you leaving food at the end of a meal dry it off as much as you can and pack it out with you in the waste bag. It has been found that burying and covering doesn't always work, animals scent it out and dig it up.

Sanitation

Please don't let your toilet paper blow about all over the place, there is no greater incentive to tear down the single track than being pursued by a windblown square of soiled Andrex. The sophistication of your toilet facilities will depend on your length of stay, but whatever happens bury it at least 20 centimetres below the surface and restore the earth above so there is absolutely no trace.

We are definitely improving in this department, a few years ago popular wilderness campsites were ringed with soggy pink toilet paper (why always pink?). The situation has improved considerably, keep up the good work.

Lichen toilet paper. Use the soft variety, you'll easily tell the difference!

It might seem a bit of a joke but there is natural toilet paper available at some locations: snow is a lot better than you may think, and soft lichens do the job quite nicely.

Trash

Pack it in, pack it out. There is no other solution. Again years ago we used to burn as much as possible then bury the cans. Unfortunately as

Duckboards on a peaty stretch of the Border Ridge in the Cheviot Hills, Northumberland, blend well in many places; virtually obscured by the reeds they focus everyone onto the same line, a great conservation measure

A well-kitted competitor approaching a checkpoint in Upper Coquetdale, Northumberland on the Polaris Challenge. He has opted to carry all his equipment on the bike which occasionally makes it difficult to lift over obstructions, but the use of the bar bag helps greatly with the balance of the machine

the numbers of us have increased this is no longer acceptable. Even remote, but regular campsites developed little areas that looked like the municipal dump, so please don't leave anything, no matter how well hidden for the time being.

You can limit your trash, and save a little weight, by removing the outer packaging of your dehydrated foods prior to departure, and the likes of Cuppasoups are usually contained in aluminised packets that are no trouble at all to take home. Don't forget a stout plastic bag for the trash.

Emergency repairs

If you suffer breakdown consider the following before launching into the mechanical aspects. Is there shelter nearby to fix it? It is amazing how quickly you cool when you stop. Unless it is the hottest day of the year put something extra on to keep warm as soon as you stop. Get out of the wind, even if it is only behind a rock or in a gulley, although the latter could be a bit cramped if you need the bike in there to work on. Walls afford excellent protection.

Is there a grass free working area? Particularly if your breakdown involves ball bearings! I once nearly picked a piece of moorland clean retrieving freewheel ball bearings that were mixed up with hailstones. Watch where you put the bits you

take off. Keep your tools wrapped in a fairly large rag, it keeps the little Allen keys safe, allows you to wipe your hands, and provides a controllable working area.

Is the weather likely to change during the repair? It might be worth walking for ten minutes to find shelter if rain threatens. It's Murphy's Law that it will start to rain as soon as you break down. How long will the repair take? If it

is only a puncture and you've got a spare tube, whip out the flat, check the tyre, remove the 'flattening agent', insert the new tyre, and you're away. If everyone mucks in it won't take long. Take the opportunity to have something to eat, it eases the pain of stopping, nuts raisins and Pedro's Lube are great!

More serious breakages pose the question 'Can I do without it?' An easy example is breaking teeth off the

Rear changers are particularly vulnerable, the short term answer is to shorten the chain and ride a single gear bike. Derailleur guards aren't the answer either, they protrude more and can shear the end completely off the axle which will reduce you to walking, even slower than a single gear special

biggest chainring, the solution is simple, only use the two smaller ones.

Listed below are **emergency self-help measures** designed to get you off the hill slowly, merely a means of making progress. It is probably advisable to get off and walk the downhills if you need to resort to some of the more extreme suggestions. Do not become a casualty yourself, you are riding a wounded bike.

Self-help list

Puncture	Thorn – remove it Snake bite – is there rim damage? Watch your fingers. Tyre casing damage – reinforce inside with patches, plastic, sticky tape, or even stitch it as Mike Tucker did on the Festive 50 some years ago. Of course you're sure to have a needle and thread!
Bent rim	Straighten as much as possible over your knee or by standing on it GENTLY. Final truing with spoke key or small adjustable spanner, then get it sorted by your wheelbuilder. Undo brake adjustment to allow it to run wobbly.
Front changer	Do without it, ride on one chainring. Stop and change rings manually. Change downover with your foot!
Rear changer	Remove broken assembly, shorten chain, ride in one gear. Middle ring, middle cog seems best. You can't use the front changer.
Handlebars	Make wooden joining spigot with your Swiss Army knife, make sure both ends are well into the handlebars. Ride VERY VERY gently. This one is only for extreme cases!
Brake lever	Tie spanner or Allen key to stump with lots of wire.
Toeclips	Do without. Remove broken bits and strap.
Chainrings	Teeth – straighten gently with small adjustable spanner. Overall buckle – gently bash with rounded stone. Remove front changer if necessary.
Pedals	Remove broken cage and ride very carefully on spindle only. Considerably safer in boots than shoes.
Pannier rack	Splint with spanner or Allen key, then bind with wire or nylon and secure with sticky tape from the first aid kit. If possible lighten the load.
Frame	Walk!

Chapter 10
Food

Food is needed for several reasons, meeting energy needs, providing essential nutrients, and helping to build damaged or dead tissue. To satisfy these demands we need a variety of foods containing: carbohydrate, fat, protein, vitamins, minerals, trace elements and water. In short a good balanced diet.

Carbohydrates provide energy, fuel for the muscles and the brain – especially important for endurance. Good sources are potatoes, rice, pasta, bread, vegetables and fruit.

Fat is much maligned but it provides fuel and is responsible to a large degree for heat production. Fish, nuts, lean meat and vegetable oils are healthy sources. Your body already has a huge energy store in the shape of fat, so there is no need to eat more, avoid fatty foods, your needs will be supplied by the hidden fats in other foods.

Protein is **the** body building material but also provides fuel, and anything up to 10% of our energy demands during prolonged exercise can be met from this source. Protein is also the source of the nine essential amino acids, but no one food can give us all of them. Good sources are fish, beans and legumes, nuts and skimmed milk. The classic beans on (brown) toast will give all nine!

Vitamins and minerals are not energy producing as such, but they are essential to the correct functioning of the body. A balanced diet should provide all the vitamins and minerals you need, however if you are really extending yourself day after day, or in serious training you will be well advised to take a diet supplement to ensure there is no deficiency.

Iron is most important mineral being responsible for the production of haemoglobin and myoglobin, which are the holders and carriers of oxygen in the blood and muscles respectively. Cycling is an aerobic exercise and demands a lot of oxygen is supplied to the muscles, so the more we can carry the better.

Make sure you get your quota. Good sources of iron are green leafy vegetables, peppers, liver, grains, nuts and supplements!

Water is the other necessity. The harder you work and the hotter the weather, the more you will need. On a hot summer's day your fluid demand could be as high as three litres, but in tropical climes you could even double that. In winter it is much less.

Summer

Your requirements will be dictated by how long you are going to be out there, you may think you don't need anything extra. Expeditions into the hills aren't a race but you will still expend a fair amount of energy, much more than normal. The odds are you won't be passing too many food emporiums, if any, so you've got to take it with you. At a certain point your body will start to convert your fat reserves to energy, but the best plan is to nibble away whenever there's an enforced stop, at a gate, or when the map's out.

We all have our favourites, some of which are the latest wonder bars, nuts and raisins, dried fruit, or even a cold jacket potato. If it is a long day, anything longer than four cycling hours, take an hour for lunch, and allow your food to be digested properly. It will save the discomfort of indigestion later.

Water is the stalwart of drinks and usually readily available in the hills, but beware the dead sheep flavour. Energy drinks come into their own when you sweat a lot, but don't mix them too strong. Many of them gum up your mouth to the point where it is uncomfortable, one answer is to take two bottles, and alternate intake with pure water.

Winter

Sweating and fluid loss is not such a problem in cold weather, but maintaining body heat is a priority. You must eat on long winter rides. Nuts and dried fruit can be supplemented by bananas, grain bars and energy drinks. Don't skimp on your breakfast if you are having an early start. If you pass a refreshment site use it, if they'll let you in, another reason for fitting mudguards, they might keep you

clean enough to be accepted at the cafe! Occasionally I carry a stove to have a hot brew. I know the calorific value of your food matters more than the heat, although hot tea or soup does have a certain extra calorific value, but the psychological value of a warm drink is immeasurable, it is worth at least 10 times its actual value, and the one-upmanship of a steam plume from your Trangia will psyche out every other biker in the shire.

The Sports Nutrition Foundation completed an interesting survey in 1992 based on the cost per 50g of carbohydrate in popular and widely available energy bars, sports drinks and supplements. Best value bar was Jordans Frusli Bar costing 69.7p/50g, followed by Prewetts Banana Bar on 80.8p, and Nesfit energy Bar at £1.02. Power Bars equated at £1.87/50g. In the drinks category Maxim was top at 35p/50gCHO, with Gatorade second on 55p and Isostar third on 68p if you used the powder and mixed your own, the tinned drinks equated at £1.68!

Expedition food

Short expeditions might well see you carrying too much food, a good fault. Only experience will tell you what you need, but with the quality of concentrated foods these days the

weight penalty of over-provision will not be great.

The following suggestions are tasty but dependent upon shops for supply, wilder expeditions demand slightly different menus, but you can always attempt to carry high energy drink/food supplements such as: Cuppasoup, Super Noodles, Beanfeast, Vesta curries usually with rice, pasta, Complan, Ovaltine – which rumour has it also helps you sleep – Maxim, energy bars, porridge, Alpine Aire mountaineering food, dried Italian pasta – high in carbohydrate.

Green tourism

Wherever you go you can support the local economy by purchasing your food when you get there, no matter what it is (within reason!).

This applies just as much at home as abroad. Needless to say on longer tours abroad you will be forced to do this, but it all helps to sustain the infrastructure and maintain a facility, no matter how primitive, for those who follow.

In remote places there might not even be shops, but like the English farmstead you will often be able to buy eggs, vegetables and milk, although these may in fact be luxuries in the depths of the Himalaya and similar regions. Simon Vickers and friends on their momentous journey across the then USSR from the Baltic to the Pacific were very much forced to live off the land, although the diet was limited to eggs, potatoes, onions, tomatoes, macaroni, unpleasant smelling tinned fish, bread, rock hard biscuits and little else. Food was hard to find in 1992 and the situation appears to be getting worse.

Such was the quality, or more accurately the lack of quality, of their diet, two of the four members of the party succumbed to exhaustion to the point where they needed medical attention, although after resting everyone completed the journey. If you are expending huge amounts of energy every day your calorific intake must be correspondingly high.

Water

In many places water can be a problem, both in purity and availability, even in areas of high precipitation such as the Alps there can be difficulties. In high summer some of the south-facing slopes dry out completely, and at other times much of the water is locked up by freezing each night, being released only when the sun reaches that particular spot. Despite the fact that it 'weighs heavy' it is good practice to keep your bottles topped up using any pure source you come across. Even in temperate climes hot days will push up your consumption to the point where larger capacity bottles are a wise investment, as are the 'lip clean' models with the huge totally enclosing caps. There is no point in seeking out pure water if you are going to drink out of a filthy neck.

Clean water

For travellers there are three ways of purifying water, boiling, tablets or filtration.

Boiling takes time, uses fuel, but often hot water is needed for dehydrated foods so it isn't a waste of energy.

Tablets are either chlorine or iodine based. The long standing Puritabs make water safe but leave it tasting slightly chlorinated, one tablet purifying one litre of water in 10 minutes. Potable Aqua, being iodine based, is more effective against a wider spectrum of bacteria than chlorine, taking the same time for the same volume, but again leaves an aftertaste.

Filters come in two basic types, those employing an activated carbon (charcoal) filter, often backed by an iodine disinfectant, and ceramic filters. There is usually a pre-filter which removes particles of sand, mud and vegetable matter, so the water looks better than the tabletted form straight away.

The flow volume is directly proportional to the size of the filter, so with the smallest filters the best plan is to do a little filtering quite often, otherwise you will spend an interminable time at the side of the stream in the evening or in the morning. If you constantly top up you will also need to carry significantly less water so will cancel out the additional weight of the filter.

Ceramics have the finest filters and the advantage that the elements can be cleaned, even the smallest Katadyn is capable of up to 100 cleansings giving it a total volume throughput of up to 4,500 litres. In comparison a similar sized charcoal or iodine system will need a new element after 400 litres, making the ceramic option essential for prolonged tours and very cost effective too.

Containers

The most advanced drinking system is the thermo-insulated Camelbak. Dirt problems are minimal and it has the added advantage of being a hands-free system. Very popular in racing circles there is no reason why it shouldn't be used on the trail too. Apparent mounting difficulties when wearing a rucksack can be overcome by stuffing it in the top pocket of your sack or even strapping it on the outside. There are no problems at all when wearing

Aline Sinclair on the summit of Bennan, Galloway, with her Camelbak secreted in her rucksack, a means of preventing freezing in sub zero temperatures — as long as the feeder tube doesn't ice up!

a bumbag. In very cold conditions the water in the tube can freeze, but in these extreme situations a bottle will probably have frozen too, the tube can soon be released by warming with the hands. Capacities are one and two litres.

Water bags are becoming more popular. The Liquipack range is based on a flexible bag with an easy to operate nozzle, and a reinforced nylon outer shell. They pack flat when not needed and come in a one-litre version which can be clipped onto a rucksack harness or a bumbag belt, and a massive seven-litre Sackpack which would be handy around camp, and of course you don't need to fill it to the top for day use.

Last word on water is the suggestion not to fill bottles or bags to capacity in the coldest weather. Freezing water can split containers, but the danger can be further lessened by taking them into the sleeping space of the tent with you where hopefully, it will be a degree or two warmer.

Emergency rations

Emergency rations should be just that. Something that will give you a boost in times of need, usually when things have gone awry due to accident, mechanical or navigational disasters. Whatever it is, it should be easy to consume. Some energy bars set solid in cold conditions and seem to require more energy to chew than what they provide. A secondary consideration is the 'shelf life' of the product. Ideally you should be able to stick it in your bumbag and forget about it until the need arises months later, then find it still in good condition. Kendal Mint Cake fulfils all these requirements, but don't eat it like sweets, it **is** supposed to be for emergencies! Ships' lifeboat rations can be a useful alternative, but again they take so much eating you need to be cast adrift for days to finish one block. The person needing sustenance could be very weak, don't finish them off with the very item intended to revive.

Chapter 11
Weather

Our lives are dominated by the weather, but why do the weather forecasters get it wrong so often? They are actually right most of the time but we don't grumble when they are, and as Bill Giles says in his excellent book *The Story of the Weather*, 'If we forecast rain and you wait long enough, it will!' Sadly the British Isles are in one of the most difficult places in the world to forecast the weather accurately to a timebase. Larger continental land masses tend to have more predictable, but often more severe weather, but wherever you travel the principles remain the same although inevitably altered by local influences.

The sun provides the energy which drives our own weather system. The phenomenal energy it gives out due to thermonuclear reactions travels in all directions and a small part of it is intercepted by the Earth. Because the Earth is tilted at 66.5° to the plane of its orbit it means that at different times of the year, first the Northern hemisphere then the Southern hemisphere gets the most sunlight, hence the seasons. But, the farthest northern latitude to have the sun directly overhead is the Tropic of Cancer at 23.5° north, at the Summer Solstice, and conversely the sun is directly above the Tropic of Capricorn, 23.5° south at the Winter Solstice in December.

From this you will appreciate that although different regions of the Earth receive similar amounts of sunlight, they do not receive similar amounts of heat. This is because the sun is directly over the Equator for most of the year and the power of the sun's rays are more concentrated. The poles, in contrast, suffer from the fact that the sun is never overhead, in fact at quite a shallow angle even at best, and the rays must pass through a thicker layer of atmosphere which further reduces their intensity and power.

If it wasn't for the fact that the warmer air at the Equator and the movement of the waters of the oceans act like a domestic central heating system, circulating the warmth, the tropics would get hotter and hotter and the Arctic and Antarctic colder and colder.

We all know that heat rises, so the simplest scenario on a grand scale would be that the hottest air, at the Equator, would rise up into the atmosphere also becoming less dense as it was heated. Air does actually have weight so as this mass rises it would create lower pressure, not quite a vacuum, but would be replaced by cooler denser air from high pressure areas like the poles, and you have the first law of meteorology, air travels from high to low pressure areas. (See Fig P)

Now enters the first complication, the rotation of the Earth. Again you'll know that the Earth is constantly spinning on its axis, at about 1,600 kph (1,000 mph) at the Equator, somewhat less as you approach the poles. As the air rises out of the Equatorial

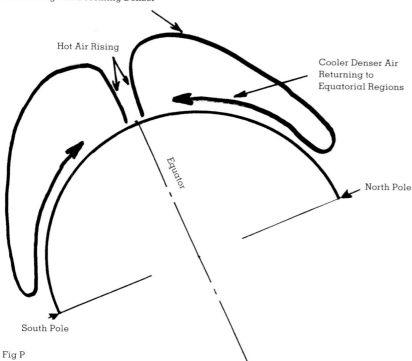

Air Cooling and Becoming Denser

Hot Air Rising

Cooler Denser Air
Returning to
Equatorial Regions

Equator

North Pole

South Pole

Fig P
Idealised airflow from Equatorial Regions

regions it is dragged to one side by the Earth's rotation. Consequently those winds generated by the hot air heading northwards towards the pole are deflected eastwards to become south westerlies. Winds are always given the name of the direction from whence they come. (See Fig Q)

Other complicating factors are the presence of large land masses, especially mountain ranges, and massive oceans which produce different effects in the weather. You

will also recall from your school physics that hot air can hold more moisture than cold, and of course once these winds and air masses start to make their way back to the Equator they are still subject to the rotational, or Coriolis effect, and what in theory could be pure northerlies become north-easterlies in the northern hemisphere.

Although some descending warm air does reach the poles from the tropics there are circulatory systems of a lesser size as you might expect,

generated by the extremes of temperature at the Equator and at the poles. These are effective over roughly a third of the Earth's latitudinal hemispheres. The hottest zone, as you will have deduced, lies from the Equator to 30° north, remember the Tropic of Cancer? with a corresponding southern equivalent, and the coldest stretch from the poles to about 60°. The other third, between 30° and 60° are the temperate zones dominated by westerly winds and associated with variable weather, and guess where the British Isles lie, dead right, on the northern edge of the northern temperate version, the collision zone, so what chance have we got? (See Fig R)

There is also the influence of the Atlantic Ocean when the winds are in the west, which they usually are, or the Eurasian continent with the vast Siberian steppes and Taiga in the east, just in case the wind changes! The only consolation we can draw is that if we were in the southern hemisphere we would be on the edge of the notorious Roaring Forties.

Sea influences

We have said ours is a temperate climate, characterised by rainfall all year round in most places, and changeable. It is largely influenced

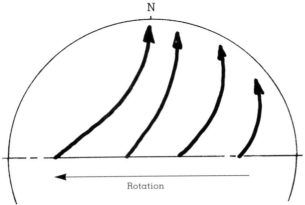

Fig Q
Hot air masses in the Northern hemisphere being deflected by the rotation of the Earth.
The Coriolis effect

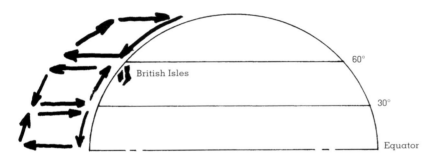

Fig R
Zonal air mass circulation in the Northern hemisphere. Note the location of the British Isles

coast, you get a really cool breeze coming in off the sea, this is generated by the rising air over the warmer land dragging colder air in from the shallow, cool North Sea which severely reduces temperatures on the coastal strip.

Worse than this are the sea fogs that occur, again usually on the east coast, when a warm stream of air passes over cold water, cooling the lower layer of air below its dew point. Known as the Haar, it can stretch well inland as it did to us on the Southern Upland Way, some 50 miles or more, and can persist for days, if the wrong sort of depression sits out in the North Sea. Fortunately this sort of inland spread only occurs in winter because in summer the sun and the heat from the land are enough to disperse the mist.

Land influences

Probably the most obvious physical influence, and the most frequently met by mountain bikers, is the effect of hills and mountains. Rain is usually caused by moisture laden air cooling, and if this air is forced upwards by a hill the likelihood is that it will cool further, so you are more likely to get rain, or at least encounter cloud on the mountain tops than in the valleys. You'll not be biking seriously very long before

by the unsettling effect of low-pressure systems moving in with the prevailing westerly or south-westerly winds from the Atlantic. This is well demonstrated by the number of times you see low after low lurking out in the North Atlantic on the forecasters' maps.

We are in a maritime temperate zone and our weather is dictated by the seas around us, which keep summer temperatures relatively cool (graphically illustrated by four inches of snow on 14 May 1993 in Kielder Forest, Northumberland!) but tempering the cold air masses approaching us in winter. Quite frequently, particularly on the east

this will become apparent, and from a safety standpoint it is essential that you are aware of this and make provision for it, for example by carrying an extra layer of clothing.

Hills also deflect the winds sideways as well as upwards turning valley rides into horrendous slogs if you are going the wrong way, or, if you are lucky, creating a protected leg that you can use to your advantage. They also create shadows, particularly on north-facing slopes, which can create extra problems especially in winter. The northern sides of mountain massifs always hold the snow longer. You don't have to go to the Alps to see this, any of your local hills will demonstrate it to some degree. Even when there is no snow about winter water could be frozen making tracks virtually impossible to ride and very dangerous.

Forecasts

From all the previous information you will now be aware of some of the problems facing the forecasters, and we never even considered the effects of gyratory high and low pressure systems, the influence of cold and warm fronts, and the huge effect of the high altitude jet stream.

Weather forecasting is a science, which is being constantly researched and improved, but I hope that this little insight has at the very least convinced you to get as up to date a forecast as possible before you set out. It is never too late to get a forecast, in fact the later the better. If you are fortunate to be going to the Scottish Highlands or the Lake District you'll be able to get an altitude related prediction on one of the special phone lines, but by constant practise you should eventually be able to hone the regional forecasts for your favourite locality to the point where at least you think you're doing a better job than the professionals.

There are several means of getting a forecast. Newspapers have the advantage of giving you a hard copy that you can compare over a number of days to see how patterns develop, but have the disadvantage of being many hours out of date simply because of the time it takes to print and distribute the papers.

Radio is pretty good because it is up to date at the time of broadcasting, but you need a receiver and are tied to precise times. Television is similar but has the advantage of pictorial displays, so at least you'll know whether your expedition will be blessed with 'single rain' or the dreaded 'double rain with splashes'!

My favourite is still the telephone forecast, they might not be as bang up to date as the broadcasting services but as you're packing the car at twenty to eight in the morning you can break off to give them a call. It's just as useful at half past seven at night in some lonely Highland glen as long as you can find a phone you can ring them, then you'll know whether to wait for sunshine tomorrow or to pack up and go home to dry out.

Jargon

It is as well to understand what some of the forecasting terms mean. They may sound very similar, but the reality is often very different for instance: isolated showers means a 10% chance of catching one; scattered showers a 30% chance; occasional showers a 50% chance.

A cold front: the leading edge of a moving air mass that is colder than the one it is replacing. Such fronts usually travel more rapidly than warm fronts, and are often accompanied by brief, heavy rain.

A warm front: the leading edge of a moving air mass that is warmer than the one it is replacing, usually accompanied by precipitation that lasts longer than the cold front.

An occluded front: forms when a cold front overtakes a warm front. Along an occluded front warm air is lifted above the ground and may shed rain or even snow for some time.

Isobar: a line on a weather map

joining points where the atmospheric pressure is the same. They tend to form circles around low pressure systems, and the closer together they lie the stronger the wind.

Instant forecasting

The professionals will tell you there is no such thing as instant forecasting, weather patterns build up over a period of days, and so they do, but for our purposes there are a few signs that may help you get your coat on before the rain comes.

Wind

Really heavy showers literally displace the air before them. On a showery day a sudden rise in wind velocity could well indicate it's time for your waterproof.

Rhododendron leaves

At normal temperatures the leaves of rhododendrons are held horizontally. As soon as the temperature drops to 2°C (35°F) the leaves begin to droop and curl, at freezing point they hang downwards, beware of ice on the tracks.

Scarlet Pimpernel

This plant closes its petals, presumably to protect its pollen from the rain, if the relative humidity rises to about 80%. Needless to say, if the petals are wide open, fine weather is set to continue. It has earned its country name: 'the poor man's weatherglass.'

Hens

often take shelter just before it rains, but if you pass through a farm they might not have any hens. How do you know whether they are sheltering or there simply aren't any? Do not go around kicking every shed to see if hens run out!

A Kestrel

hovering low over the ground indicates showery or blustery weather on the way. He is anxiously hunting for mice before the weather deteriorates.

Sheep

In hilly districts they will come down to the low lying land shortly before the arrival of snow, so if you meet them coming down of their own accord as you are going up, turn back.

Cattle

often lie down just before the arrival of rain, or huddle together in the fields or in the shelter of hedges with their bums to the wind shortly before the arrival of wet and windy weather.

Finally, from hilltop vantage points you can often see rain or snow approaching. Take the appropriate action. Get off the tops.

Weather lore

There are many sayings or poems that forecast the weather. How do they stand up to close examination?

'Rainbow at morn, good weather has gone.
Rainbow after noon, good weather comes soon.'

Rainbows are caused by the sun's rays passing through raindrops and being refracted in the process, causing the white light to split into its constituent parts – red, orange, yellow, green, blue, indigo and violet. To see a rainbow you must be standing between the sun and the rain. The best examples are seen when the sun is low in the sky, morning or early evening. 'Rainbow at morn,' because the sun will be in the east the rainbow must be in the west, and if the wind is westerly, which after all is the prevailing wind, the sun will be shining on drops of moisture approaching from the west. Rain is on the way. 'Rainbow after noon,' on this occasion the rainbow must be in the east. The rain has gone. It works, unless of course the wind is easterly!

'Mountains in the morning,
Fountains in the evening.'

Mackerel sky portending bad weather

Winter stratus being shredded by the wind among the hills, no precipitation. Eskdale, Cumbria, November

A build up of billowy white cumulus clouds gives warning of approaching thunderstorms, often the same day. If the cumulus clouds assume large proportions and flatten out at the top into an anvil shape, thunder is certain somewhere.

'Trace in the sky the painter's brush,
And winds around you soon will rush.'

Wispy cirrus clouds, often referred to as mare's tails, the highest clouds in the sky, foretell approaching winds. Their height dictates that they are made up of ice crystals which give them their distinctive appearance. Cirro stratus are also high altitude clouds, and as the second part of the name suggests, they are layer clouds that cover much of the sky. They often herald bad weather and produce a halo effect around the sun or moon, which people have used for centuries as a sign of rain.

'Mackerel sky and mare's tails,
Make tall ships carry low sails.'

Invariably an indicator of an approaching warm front and a strengthening of the winds.

'Red sky at night, shepherd's delight.
Red sky at morning, shepherd's
warning.'

The sun sets in the west and shining up onto a cloud layer to give

Weather signs: rolling dense clouds over the three peaks, Ribblesdale, West Yorkshire, September. There's no rain, but it could go either way

the distinctive glowing red, it can signify that a front, which produces rain, has passed. The reverse is the case with the sun rising in the east in the morning. However, it is still a lot safer to rely on the BBC forecast at 2130 hours, even for shepherds and mountain bikers!

Wind

Wind strength and direction can either make or break your day. Very often the direction or the strength, or both, will change during your ride. Find out what it is likely to do and plan accordingly. When travelling abroad find out whether there are any regular winds such as the Mediterranean Mistral, the Khamsin or the Sirocco that may affect your plans.

Your route will often start and finish at the same point but it is highly unlikely that it will be circular in shape, more probable will be a triangular course. By taking into account the wind direction and strength forecast it should be possible to minimise the pain of the windward leg and use the wind to your advantage late in the day when you are likely to be most tired. Fig S shows a likely route, study it and decide your tactics.

Wind speed

Increasingly wind speeds are being

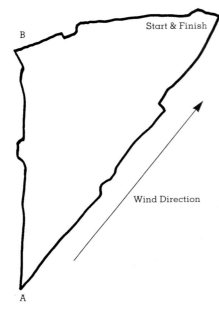

B

Start & Finish

Wind Direction

A

Fig S
Typical day route with wind direction.
Consider all the options to minimise the
pain of the windward legs, or legs!

Sample route taking note of wind direction

Forecast: light wind from the south west increasing in strength during the afternoon.

Option 1: start at 1000 hours. Attack the windward leg to point A when you are fresh and get it out of the way before the wind strength increases. The other two legs will then have the wind more or less at your back.

Option 2: travel to point B first, then south to point A when the wind is at its weakest, then, as it strengthens have it at your back and get blown home in the afternoon.

Option 3: make an early start, say 0830 hours, and repeat Option 2, making sure you complete two legs. Start to B, and B to A, before the wind achieves any appreciable strength at all. This should be even easier than Option 2.

Of course topography will play a major role in the plan too. It is possible to ride downhill into most winds, but uphill over rough terrain into any wind can reduce you to walking.

---

shown on pictorial forecasts in mph or kph, but the shipping forecast and many others still use the Beaufort Scale. The scale was drawn up by Sir Francis Beaufort, an admiral of the British Navy, to denote the speed of the wind, giving each range of speed a number that corresponded to the amount of sail a man-of-war would carry in such a wind. The chart shows what these mean speed wise, the physical signs and potential damage.

Wind sense
Never underestimate the wind. Hills are obstructions that will naturally accelerate any wind by causing it to rise over them or push around the sides. Try to anticipate gaps or cols where gusts might tear through, and be prepared to dismount in extreme cases. A further complication is that the shape of the immediate hills can funnel wind from a different, unexpected direction, and these local high speed gusts can be severe enough to take the bike from

underneath you. If in doubt get off and walk.

Battling into a wind can be exhausting. Keep a close eye on lighter or weaker members of the party who will be most affected by the constant buffeting.

Wind chill
On dry cold days air temperature and wind speed combine to cause the cooling effect known as wind chill. For any given air temperature the wind chill factor increases

Snow can be ridden, provided it's the right type. Frozen, compacted, and relatively smooth, but how would you fancy the 200 mile Iditabike race in Alaska. You will need to be supremely fit, highly competent, and well equipped

Iditabike race, Alaska. Real arctic conditions, but two riding together providing mutual support, and well kitted out including head torches as darkness approaches

The Beaufort wind scale

Beaufort Force No	Average Speed MPH	Average Speed KPH	Description	Physical Signs
0	0	0	Calm	Smoke rises vertically
1	2	3	Light airs	Smoke drifts in the wind
2	5	9	Light breeze	Leaves rustle
3	10	15	Gentle breeze	Leaves and small twigs move constantly. Small flags extended
4	15	25	Moderate wind	Wind raises dust and small paper
5	21	35	Fresh wind	Small trees sway
6	28	45	Strong wind	Large branches move. Whistling in phone wires. Difficult to use umbrellas
7	35	56	Very strong wind	Whole trees in motion
8	43	68	Gale	Twigs break off trees. Difficult to walk
9	50	81	Severe gale	Chimney pots and slates removed
10	59	94	Storm	Trees uprooted. Structural damage
11	69	110	Severe storm	Widespread damage
12	over 74	over 119	Hurricane	Widespread damage

rapidly with increasing wind speed. This is most pronounced at lower wind speeds, so that in the range 0-24kph (0-15mph) even small changes in wind speed have a profound effect on the degree of cooling. Take heed, we can produce this effect by simply riding along!

Strangely, at wind speeds above 24kph the factor changes more slowly, but this does not mean that high winds can be discounted. As already mentioned a great deal more energy is required to fight against a strong wind.

Wind chill is a major cause of mountain hypothermia. Take precautions. Put all your clothing on for descents on cold days, especially your windproof shell: this should prevent rapid cooling and the onset of chills, and will also give extra protection should you crash onto frozen ground.

Quick changes

Even the local weather forecast is a few hours out of date, but when you are up in the hills you can literally see it happening. Once you develop your recognition skills you will be able to take the appropriate action in ample time. Act before the change hits you.

The most obvious action is to don extra clothing as appropriate – usually your waterproofs. Getting off the hill is the correct response to severe weather. You should always carry the appropriate OS map to find the best escape route. Having said that, don't flee for the valley at the first opportunity, you might be taking yourself into more trouble. Consider the alternatives, mistakes can be very costly in time and effort when riding high.

Taking shelter is the less drastic option, but shelter is usually hard to find. Many well-frequented routes have mountain rescue posts, usually huts, which are an excellent refuge; you can sometimes find shelter in caves, gullies, cairns, or simply getting into the lee of the hill or finding a hollow.

If you decide to flee the tops it is not unusual to find yourself minutes later in the relative calm and warmth of the valley, feeling a bit soft, but there is no finer illustration of 'better safe than sorry'. People have perished by trying to keep going at all costs. The beauty of the mountain bike is that you can get off the hill very quickly. In this department it is quite supreme.

Poor visibility

Cloud or mist can appear on the finest of days. Even in summer moisture laden air forced upwards by the hills can start to form mist as it comes towards you. Clouds usually roll down the hill at you, or loiter waiting for you to climb up into them. They are a trap for the unwary.

The obvious thing to do in poor visibility is to slow down, or even get off and walk. That way you will not charge into anything, or anyone. Goggles or glasses will soon be covered in water droplets, take them off immediately.

The other alternative is to take a rest until the cloud lifts, but this is not very attractive. Who wants to take a break sitting in cloud with no view, and it will be very cold and damp too. The best thing to do is to keep moving slowly, so long as you don't wander off course. If the trail is difficult to follow there is no alternative, don all available clothing and wait.

Lightning

There is probably more folklore about lightning than any other facet of the weather, but it can hardly be regarded as a major mountain hazard. On the other hand it would be ridiculous to ignore it.

Strikes tend to be concentrated on mountain tops, trees or other natural projections, so if you are riding on a ridge at the time of an electrical storm it makes sense to get off if possible, and go at least part of the way down.

In the past you would have been advised to discard metal objects like cameras or rucksacks with steel buckles, in the belief they attract lightning. They don't, any more than you do, but a bike is a fair mass of metal, and if it starts humming or sparking, which could happen if you are riding really high, set it down some distance away. You shouldn't need any prompting to do this! Don't heave it over a cliff, it is far too expensive a bit of kit to destroy, and when the storm passes you'll need it to flee to the valley.

Darkness

Riding off-road in the dark can be very dangerous on unfamiliar tracks, or perhaps even more so on pistes you know well! The safest thing to do is avoid doing it, but serious mountain bikers are bound to do it, or more honestly forced to do it, often on winter routes when we run out of daylight. In preparation for the inevitable it is sensible to try it in a controlled environment, or as controlled as off-road riding can be. Try your lighting set up in total darkness and refine it to your needs.

Lighting systems

Not many of us have our lights fitted permanently, or at least the batteries, because an effective off-road system requires a lot of lumens which in turn demand a beefy battery. Critics of bike mounted lights quite rightly make the point that many set ups succumb to excessive vibration and often don't point where you want to look, but a well-set up twin headlight arrangement should cover virtually all eventualities, and perform equally as well as a head torch.

Head torches like Petzl lights are good, they point exactly where you look, and can be used around camp too. The disadvantages are lack of depth of beam which restricts your speed, which might not be a bad thing! On the odd occasion when it snows, if you are caught out in a blizzard you will find that all that is illuminated are the snowflakes immediately in front of your face, which is a total disaster, and the sole reason for me changing to a bike mounted system. Having said this a head torch is reasonably light in weight and can be carried for emergency use.

Night sight

Even if you are caught out without any sort of illumination all is not lost, no doubt you will have gradually come into this situation, and should get your 'night sight' without any trouble. It is amazing how much you can actually see, but please be careful, beware of any black patches, they could be bottomless holes or Galloway cattle! Snow on the ground is an enormous help, reflecting any light source, but hiding some of the holes. You have been warned.

The danger of being really fit and battle hardened, especially in the egocentric male, is a lack of humility in the face of impossible odds. We've all done it, not only flaunted the limits but stepped across the sensibility line, most of us got away with it and learned a valuable lesson, others didn't and paid the ultimate price. You must have confidence in your ability, but an overwhelming conceit is downright deadly.

No matter how fit and hard you are occasions might arise when it is folly to continue with an injury. Very often it is harder to quit than continue, don't duck the decision, you may put others at risk by pressing on. It's the same with illness. If you are feeling unwell don't go on unless there is no alternative, return when you recover. Concentration goes when you're feeling grotty and you could do more damage to yourself by coming off.

Try to keep yourself germ and injury free. This means taking a deliberate decision to ride within your capabilities when you're out in the wilds, especially if the bike and you are carrying extra load.

Hypothermia

You are just as likely to encounter hypothermia in your local hills as anywhere else. It is most dangerous to those who don't know what it is. Hypothermia is caused by cold. The core of your body cools gradually, and your functions begin to slow down and stop. Symptoms vary from mild confusion, lack of co-ordination and lethargy to coma. Occasionally people act in a strange manner, doing silly things such as shouting and swearing out of character. The first problem you face is persuading the sufferer that something is wrong.

Causes

One of the main causes of mountain hypothermia is windchill which occurs in a dry, cold environment; it follows that good windproof clothing is essential in these conditions.

The greatest number of cases in the UK occur as a result of being wet and cold. Modern fabrics and garment design are going a long way to help in this direction, but ensure you are well kitted out for high altitude or winter riding. (See Chapter 4 Apparel)

Exhaustion is another cause, brought on by a lack of training, attempting too much, or not eating sufficient. In cold conditions the demands you make of your body can become quite excessive, especially if they are maintained for any length of time. A good balanced diet is essential, including high-energy drinks or snacks to be taken *en route*.

Dehydration can also be a cause: drink little and often, even in winter, you expel a huge amount of water by simply breathing, even more when engaged in serious effort, just because you're not sweating so much doesn't mean you're not using water. If you need convincing check how much condensation or frost has accumulated on the **inside** of your tent in the mornings, and that is produced when you are at rest. When active your body requires even more fluid!

Illness and injury heighten the risk of hypothermia. Shock is present to some degree in every case of injury, and a person in a state of shock is much less able to combat the effects of cold and maintain their body temperature. In fact they are well on the way towards hypothermia, keep them warm by any means at your disposal.

Symptoms

Initially feeling cold or tired, but most of us experience the latter at some stage of the day, don't dismiss it, keep it at the back of your mind. Gradually other symptoms develop, you may experience some or all of these:

- Numbness of hands and feet and intermittent bouts of shivering, but again you might experience the former on severe climbs or descents, especially in the Alps.
- Uncontrollable shivering indicates a serious state of affairs.
- Muscle cramps.
- Unexpected or unreasonable

behaviour! (Not in mountain bikers, surely!)
- Both physical and mental lethargy.
- Light headedness.
- Failing to understand or answer questions.
- Extreme ashen pallor.
- Some slurring of speech.
- Violent outbursts of both language and/or energy.
- Erratic movements, more falling off than usual.
- Difficulty in focussing. If this occurs the condition should be regarded as extremely serious – act fast.
- Fainting

These symptoms will not necessarily occur in this order or you may not recognise them immediately, keep your eye on one another, especially the younger members of the party.

The British Mountaineering Council (BMC) recommends the following for prevention and treatment:

Prevention

'Be adequately prepared for the conditions you are likely to encounter. Don't forget that a large proportion of your body heat escapes from your head – 'If you want to keep your feet warm, wear a hat!' and effective wind and waterproof clothing. It is important to maintain a reasonable food intake, particularly of high energy foods containing

carbohydrate. In improvised shelters or a tent, adequate insulation from the ground is very important in preventing further deterioration from cold. If possible avoid getting wet and seek or improvise shelter early if conditions are deteteriorating, as exhaustion accelerates the effects of cold. If one member of a party develops exhaustion hypothermia, other members may soon develop the same – so take decisive action early rather than late.

Treatment

'If practical, remove wet clothing and replace with dry. Warm slowly. If the temperature is very low, rapid rewarming may cause fatal cardiac arrythmias. Wrapping in a space blanket inside a sleeping bag is as good as anything if more elaborate facilities are not available. If trapped out in extreme conditions, get friendly and share your heat with the victim by sharing a bag. Hypothermia victims are often dehydrated and so if they are conscious, encourage fluid intake. If available, intravenous fluids are helpful when the victim is unconscious. To have the best outlook, profound hypothermia needs specialist treatment – if in doubt get help.'

If you are in a party of mountain bikers include these:

- if there is no cover form a human shield, give moral support
- recovery might be quite quick, 30 minutes or so, but don't move off until you are sure recovery is complete
- don't press on regardless, escape in safety is now the name of the game
- share the victim's load, it could have benefits for all of you in the long run.

Effects of heat

Exposure to heat is a rare occurrence in northern Europe and the British Isles, but those fortunate to migrate south to the warmer climes of the Mediterranean countries and farther afield to enjoy not only the climate but also some supreme mountain biking, need to be aware of the effects.

Most heat related disorders are due to water depletion. The average daily requirement is about two and a half to three litres per day, but this is greatly increased by hard physical effort, and in really hot conditions demand may rise to eight litres per day.

Precautions

Acclimatisation happens very quickly but a wise plan is to drink more water than you need when it is readily available, and to avoid prolonged exertion in the heat of the day. Stay in the shade as much as possible initially, build up your exposure to strong sunlight gradually. Ride early and late, rising at first light and doing the bulk of the day's mileage in the cool of the morning. Evening riding tends to be more limited due to the heating effect of the day.

Sunburn is the other obvious threat, even in northern climes. At high altitude the atmosphere is much thinner and provides less protection from ultraviolet rays. This will be noticeable at anything over 2,000m. Invest in a strong sunscreen and use it liberally. Any pre-expedition build up of tan is worth it. There is also a risk of sunburn on bright sunny days in winter when snow is on the ground, protect the undersides of your chin, nose and eyebrows, and don't forget your shades. Old-fashioned calamine lotion is still a good treatment for sunburn.

Salt requirements

Normally our daily salt intake is far beyond our requirements, but prolonged sweating will lead to substantial loss, especially if you are not fully acclimatised. About two grammes of salt is lost for every litre of fluid loss, but the immediate effects can be countered by taking salt tablets or a solution. Cutting down on water intake will also help, but water or salt depletion can lead to heat exhaustion which will only be alleviated by re-establishing the balance.

Heatstroke

Often referred to as sunstroke, this occurs when your normal temperature regulating mechanism can't cope and your body overheats. The victim will have a very high temperature, may be confused and delirious and their skin is often flushed and dry. Heatstroke can be fatal. The condition is usually brought on by too much exercise in a hot climate, coupled with an inadequate fluid intake. Humid conditions can accelerate the effect by preventing sweat from evaporating and cooling the body.

Treatment is **urgent**. Get the victim into the shade, cover them with wet towels or cloths, and fan vigorously. Encourage them to drink plenty of fluids. If there is a cold bath available, immerse the victim in it.

Mountain rescue

Not so very long ago there were few mountain rescue teams and no helicopters. The original team, the

RAF Mountain Rescue, set up to recover their own personnel, are still at the forefront with the terrific men of the Search And Rescue Units, but they have many responsibilities and should not be summoned lightly.

Not so long ago all mountain bike race regulations had a clause which said 'competitors should be self sufficient for both machine and rider', this is a principle that should always apply in the mountains. You should set off with the clear understanding that you are in fact self sufficient, and be prepared to help anyone else, biker, walker, climber or horse rider, who needs your assistance.

Accidents

Long distance adventurers cannot afford to have accidents, their big objective is to complete the challenge with a minimum of distractions. If your preparation and planning is aimed at making sure they won't happen you can reduce the possibility considerably. But of course, accidents can never be eliminated, always allow for the unexpected.

When planning your riding for the day, always mark the nearest sources of help and how to get there. Never skimp on maps, get the most detailed and accurate maps available, that way the information will probably be there already. Know what to do in case of serious injury, how many will stay with the casualty, how many go for help, don't leave all the decisions until panic has set in. If an accident does occur, keep the lid on it, don't let it get out of hand.

Make sure you have the supplies and equipment to cope with an emergency. In the Sahara for example your only course might be to get to the lorry route and wait for a truck. Have you got enough water for 48 hours?

Simple first aid

There is no substitute for professional medical help or proper first aid training. Enrol on a course run by one of the organisations listed below as soon as possible - you might be able to do it through work or college. Until then the advice in this chapter will help, but if you come across anything you can't cope with leave it alone, you could do more harm than good.

St John Ambulance; St Andrew's Ambulance Association; British Red Cross, all run courses and have a good first aid manual. Look up their local headquarters in the telephone directory and they will advise the most suitable course.

The aims of first aid are: to preserve life, to limit the effects of the injury or condition, and to promote recovery. Saving life is the priority. Worrying about spinal injuries will do no good if the victim is not breathing and has no heartbeat. The brain dies if deprived of oxygen for more than three minutes, so if someone is not breathing or has no circulation, this is the time limit within which you **must act**.

Checklist

Dial 999 for an ambulance. Great if you are half way up a mountain, but can anyone be sent to set the wheels in motion while you attend to the casualty?

Check for danger to you or the casualty.

Is the casualty conscious?

Go into the ABC routine (see later)Treat any life threatening injury. Treat wounds and breakages as appropriate.

Do not remove a crash helmet unless absolutely necessary, or the casualty can do it themselves, or it is interfering with resuscitation.

This is the BMC's guideline for saving life. The easy way to remember it is ABC: A (airway) B (breathing) C (circulation)

Airway Ensure the airways in and out are not blocked. With your fingers clear the back of the throat of blood, vomit, false teeth, or anything else that may have been in the mouth at the moment of falling.

The commonest object to block the airway is the tongue which, in somebody unconscious and lying on their back, tends to sag to the back of the throat. (In somebody who is attempting to breath this will cause a choking noise.) Put your fingers behind the angle of the jaw, on each side of the head, and pull the tongue forward until air is going in and out without hindrance.

Breathing If the casualty is not breathing, commence mouth to mouth resuscitation, highly unpleasant if the victim has just vomited, but are you going to let them die just because they're smelly? It's not much worse than drinking out of a muddy water bottle! Use a water bottle to wash them down a little.

Tilt the patient's head back, pinch the nostrils shut (otherwise your breath goes straight back out, rather than into their lungs), take a breath, put your mouth over theirs and breath out strongly. Watch the chest carefully. If it rises as you blow air in and falls as you let the air come out, you're doing it properly. You don't need to suck the air back out as the lungs contain elastic-like

material and automatically deflate like a balloon. You should be breathing into an adult about 12 times a minute. Don't stop until they start to breath for themselves.

Circulation Don't waste time trying to listen for a heartbeat, check out the pulse in the neck, the carotid artery, straight away.' Check it out on yourself NOW, as you read this, between the Adam's Apple and the strap muscle. Use two fingers. The pulse may be very weak in someone who has just sustained an injury, but if you can't find a pulse in the neck start cardiac massage immediately. This is something else, like mouth to mouth resuscitation, that needs to be practised to be done well.

These are procedures involved at the severe end of the scale of injury, and require techniques that are taught on first aid courses.

If you are prepared then you can you do something to help instead of standing by helpless in the event of an accident.

Most other procedures are simple by comparison, and what follows here is of secondary importance, although essential in most cases.

Safety

Make the area safe. If the injured rider has come off riding down a boulder strewn gully he may have loosened a huge rock that is poised to tumble down onto you both. If

you cannot eliminate the danger, try to put some distance between it and the casualty. This is an on the spot decision, but do not move the casualty unless absolutely necessary.

Comfort

Make the casualty as comfortable as possible, often this involves keeping them warm, especially out in the hills. Riders who have been injured are more susceptible to hypothermia. Don't forget to insulate them from the ground, there is little point in lashing extra clothes onto their torso if their bum's freezing. Sit or lie them on non-porous material, padded and made warmer with a fleece, even a polythene bag will help.

Try to get them into a sheltered spot if they can walk, but if there is any hint of a spinal injury leave them where they are until specialist help arrives. You could try building a temporary windbreak from whatever materials are available. Never move a casualty alone, unless there is only you there. Explain to the victim what you are doing, so they can assist if they are able.

If there is more than one person involved in moving the casualty make sure only one rescuer gives the commands. Try not to get the giggles, it is amazing how quickly confusion can quickly degenerate into farce. It is one thing reassuring and relaxing the casualty, it is another aggravating their injuries with laughter. Keep a lid on it.

Messengers

Mountain bikers have a huge advantage over just about everyone else in the hills in that we travel faster, especially downhill, and that is invariably the direction to travel to seek help, but don't go so fast that you too become a casualty. You will be excited and tense, so control yourself. The most important thing is that you get there. If you are going to act as messengers, travel as a pair if you can.

Get first hand information. If it is one of your party that is injured you will know the situation, but if your help is needed by another party make sure you get the best information available. If the accident is close by, go back and check what has happened. It is quite common for other members of the party to act irrationally. Second hand information may be exaggerated or something important may be omitted. If at all possible write it down. You need:

Message details
1 Precise details of the accident, including what time it occurred.
2 Location with map reference.
3 Number of casualties with names if possible.

4 Nature of injuries and details of any help at the scene.
5 What is the rest of the party doing? Are they staying with the casualty, or bringing him/her out slowly?
6 Any relevant information about the terrain. Which way did you come out, and which way will the casualty be moving? Take good notice of your route out, you may be required to guide the rescue team back in the dark.
7 Estimated time of arrival of the casualty at the nearest road for the ambulance.
8 Act speedily, not hastily. Inform the local police and ambulance by 999, they will make the rescue arrangements. Be prepared to stand by the telephone.

If your map doesn't show it, look for the first building with telephone wires going to it, often a farmhouse. A telephone kiosk might be miles down the road, but if it is, the mountain bikers will cover the ground quickest.

Summoning help

Help required is signalled either by red flares, by six blasts in quick succession on a whistle, or six flashes in quick succession on a torch.

Signals for communicating with rescue helicopters are usually laid down by the official rescue team, but it may be down to you. The signs and symbols should be at least three metres in size using whatever contrasting materials come to hand, rocks, clothing, bracken or even rucksacks.

Fig T

 Safe to land here

 Require a doctor

 Proceeding in the direction of the arrow

 Unable to proceed

 Nothing found

 Require medical supplies

 Require assistance

 All well

The pilot will select a safe area to land. If a marker of any kind is used it should be firmly weighted down. Clear away loose debris, and keep well clear to the windward because the helicopter will approach into the wind. Making smoke, without setting the whole moor alight, will be of great assistance to the pilot. Do not approach the helicopter until signalled to do so by a member of the crew, then do exactly as you are told. Remember the rescue is for you only, not your bike, unless of course the pilot is a mountain biker too!

Evacuation by bike

You can do more damage to a casualty by bringing them out on a bike than has already been done. I am tempted to say 'Don't do it', but I know you will, because I have. Just do it carefully.

Wrist and arm injuries are common. Don't ride over rough ground with one hand, you'll just fall off. Consider swapping the brakes around to ensure the good hand is operating the **rear** brake. Again I speak from painful experience. I started off with a sprained wrist and elbow lacerations and finished with broken ribs and a gashed leg too!

Only give a 'backer' on smooth roads. Apart from the obvious dangers on the rocky bits, it could break your bike.

Bibliography

Stretching
Bob Anderson, Pelham Books 1981

Animal Tracks and Signs
Preben Bang and Preben Dahlstrom, Collins 1974

First Aid on Mountains
Steve Bollen MB FRCS, British Mountaineering Council 1989

Ancient Pathways in the Alps
Giovanni Caselli and Keith Sugden, George Philip & Son 1988

Weather
John Farrand Jr, Stewart, Tabori & Chang 1988

Weatherwise
Bill Foggitt, Pavilion Books

The Story of the Weather
Bill Giles, HMSO/Shell UK 1992

Mountain bike racing
Tim Gould and Simon Burney, Springfield Books 1992

Soft Paths
Bruce Hampton and David Cole, Stackpole Books 1988

Mountaincraft and Leadership
Eric Langmuir, Scottish Sports Council 1984

Heading for the Scottish Hills
Mountaineering Council of Scotland and the Scottish Landowners Federation, Scottish Mountaineering Trust 1988

Mountain Weather
David Pedgley, Cicerone Press 1980

First Aid Manual
St John Ambulance, St Andrew's Ambulance Association, British Red Cross, Dorling Kindersley 1992

Rights of Way – A Guide to the Law in Scotland
Scottish Rights of Way Society, 1991

Between the Hammer and the Sickle: Across Russia by Bike
Simon Vickers, Sinclair Stevenson 1992

Guides and guide books

Some of the guidebooks listed relate specifically to long distance paths, however they all contain sections of unclassified road or bridleway which can legally be used by cyclists.

England

Derbyshire & Peak District Mountain Bike Guide
Tim Banton, Andy Spencer, Tom Windsor, Ernest Press 1993

Lake District, Howgills & Yorkshire Dales Mountain Bike Guide
Jeremy Ashcroft, Ernest Press 1989

More Routes in the Lake District, Howgills & Yorkshire Dales MTB Guide
Jeremy Ashcroft, Ernest Press 1993

Northumberland Mountain Bike Guide
Derek Purdy, Ernest Press 1993

Peddars Way & Norfolk Coast Path
Bruce Robinson, Aurum Press 1992

The Ridgeway
Neil Curtis, Aurum Press 1992

Wolds Way
Roger Ratcliffe, Aurum Press 1992

West Yorkshire Mountain Bike Guide
Ernest Press 1993

Scotland
Exploring Scottish Hill Tracks
Ralph Storer, David & Charles 1991

Great Walks – Scotland
Hamish Brown, Rennie McOwan, Richard Mearns, Ward Lock 1989

Southern Upland Way
Ken Andrew, HMSO 1984

Wales
Offa's Dyke Path South
Ernie & Kathy Kay, Mark Richards, Arum Press 1989

France
Tour de Mont Blanc
Andrew Harper, Cicerone Press 1977

Walking Europe from Top to Bottom, Grande Randonnee Cinq (GR5)
Susanna Margolis, San Francisco Sierra Club 1986
Walking in France
Rob Hunter, Hamlyn 1983

Germany
Mountain Biking (Bavaria)
Elmar Moser, German text, Off Editions 1989

Holland
Cycling In Holland
Netherlands Tourist Board

Switzerland
Guide Suisse De Mountain Bike (French/German text) D S Edition

North America
Colorado High: The Official Guide to the Colorado Trail
Randy Jacobs, Free Solo Press 1988

Hiking Trails in Southwestern Colorado
Paul Pixler, Pruett 1981

Useful Addresses

British Mountain Bike Federation
36 Rockingham Road, Kettering,
Northamptonshire NN16 8HG
Tel: 0536 412211

British Trust for Conservation
Volunteers
36 St. Mary's Street, Wallingford,
Oxfordshire OX10 0EU
Tel: 0491 39766

British Waterways Board
Melbury House, Melbury Terrace,
London NW1 6JX
Tel: 071 7258005

Federation Francais de la
Randonnee Pedestre
Comite National des Sentiers de
Grande Randonnee,
92 rue de Clignancourt, 75883 Paris,
France

Forest Enterprise and Forestry
Commission
231 Corstorphine Road, Edinburgh,
Midlothian EH12 7AT
Tel: 031 3340303

Royal Geographical Society
Expedition Advisory Centre,
1 Kensington Gore, London
SW7 2AR
Tel: 071 5895466

Scottish Cyclists' Union
The Velodrome, Meadowbank
Stadium, London Road, Edinburgh
EH7 6AD
Tel: 031 6520187

Scottish Rights of Way Society
Unit 2, John Cotton Business
Centre, 10 Sunnyside, Edinburgh
EH7 5RA
Tel: 031 6522937

Sports Nutrition Foundation
National Sports Medicine Institute
of the UK, c/o Medical College of
St Bartholomew's Hospital,
Charterhouse Square, London
EC1M 6BQ
Tel: 071 2500493

Map Suppliers

A T Atkinson & Partner,
The Map Shop
15 High Street, Upton-on Severn
Worcs WR8 0HJ
Tel: 0684 593146 Fax: 0684 594559

Edward Stanford Ltd
12-14 Long Acre, Covent Garden,
London WC2E 9LP
Tel: 071 836 1321
Fax: 071 836 0189

Heffers Bookshop
19 Sidney Street,
Cambridge CB2 3HL
Tel: 0223 358241

Index

climbing 37
protein 129
punctures 128
Purdy, Graeme 99
Puritabs 131

R
rain 136
rear changer 11, 127, 128
relating speed to terrain 58
repairs to pannier rack 115
Ridgeway, the 67
Rockrings 24
rocky outcrop, map marking 83
Roddam Rigg 62
routine for camping 116
rucksacks 112

S
saddles 11
    adjustment 10
    gel 14
    leather 14
    position 11–12
    tilt 12
safety
sanitation, when camping 124
Scotland, recommended areas 69
    rights of way 62
scree, map marking 83
seatpost 12
shelters 104
Shimano SPD 14
Shocktechs 14
sill water 32
Simpson, Jane 14
Sinclair, Aline 132
sleeping bags 122
sleeping mats 123
snow 143
Southern Upland Way Approach
(see Wetland Way Approach)
Spain, recommended areas 70

spares, carrying 16
Specialized tyres 27
specialist materials 45
speed 26
Spence, Alex 32, 37, 111
sphagnum stopper 24
stells 56
stem height 11
Stevenson, Robert Louis 77
stoves 123
summoning help 153
Superflate Speedpump 16
survival blanket 16
suspension units 14, 34
Swinhope Moor 95
Switzerland, recommended areas 73

T
Tarn Beck Bothy 105
technique and innovation 27
tents 116
terrain, changes to 58–59
Thirlwall Common 77
Threlkeld Common, Cumbria 66
Thompson, Brian 67
thumbshifters 11, 13
toeclips 14, 37, 50, 128
Tomkins, Pete 15, 27
tool kit checklist 17
top tube reach 10
track hazards 20
trackmitts 14
trailcraft 26
training, hills 38–39
    record 52
    basic programme 54
trash disposal 124–127
Trek Shoulder Holder 38
tube protection 38
tyres 11
    choosing 27
twin headlights 15

U
Upper Coquetdale 100, 126
using a compass 85

V
V of river 100, 101
Vickers, Simon 25, 130
vitamins 129
voluntary restrictions on rights of way
    64

W
Wales, recommended areas 68
    rights of way 60
walkers 66
Waskerley Way, Co Durham 29
Watendlath, Cumbria 31
water, bottle 11
    containers 131
    purifying 131
waterproofs 47
weather lore 138
weight, bike 16
    rider 26
    shedding 39
West Coldside, Northumberland 32
Wetland Way approach 56
wheels 11
whistle 16
Wilderness camping 119
Wilks, Glen 14, 29, 56
Williams, Malcolm 99
Willyshaw Rigg 24
wind, chill 142
    speed 141
Wooler Water, Coldgate Mill 32

Y
Yair, Borders Region 41